D0542645

ENGINE SHEDS
IN CAMERA

DAVID HUCKNALL

SUTTON PUBLISHING

First published in 2005 by
Sutton Publishing Limited · Phoenix Mill
Thrupp · Stroud · Gloucestershire · GL5 2BU

British Library Cataloguing in Publication Data
A catalogue record for this book is available from the British Library.

ISBN 0-7509-4191-X

Title page photograph: 'Castle' Class No. 5029 *Nunney Castle* is seen at Didcot on 9 June 1991. Everything
about the locomotive and its presentation reflects creditably on those who carefully restore and care
for the remaining steam locomotives in Britain.

Typeset in 10/12 pt Palatino.
Typesetting and origination by
Sutton Publishing Limited.
Printed and bound in England by
J.H. Haynes & Co. Ltd, Sparkford.

Contents

Introduction   5

Acknowledgements   6

1. A Selection of Sheds   7

2. Inside   31

3. Preparation/Disposal   49

4. In the Yard   73

5. The Men   87

6. Portraits   101

7. Duties   121

8. The End   131

Appendix   139

Bibliography   142

Index   143

One of the preparation/disposal men at St Margarets shed, having finished the dirty and uncomfortable task of removing char from the smokebox of V2 Class No. 60931, prepares to dismount the locomotive on 17 April 1965. Smokebox char contained fine, abrasive material that could find its way into the clothing and boots of the P and D man. It had to be dug out of the smokebox and thrown well clear of the engine. Afterwards, the door sealing face had to be cleaned, the very heavy smokebox door shut and the running plate swept. Judging by the amount of material that had been removed, 60931 had been worked extremely hard, possibly with poor fuel, on its previous duty. *(D.J. Hucknall)*

Introduction

In 1997, a compilation of all steam locomotive sheds of the passenger-carrying railways of England, Scotland and Wales from 1825 to 1968 indicated that there were approximately 2,250 where it is 'known or strongly believed' that engines or enginemen were stationed. It would clearly be a daunting task to deal with the wealth and variety of information that exists on the structures that have been used to house and service locomotives. In the case of LMS engine sheds, however, an attempt has been made in the form of the thorough and excellent summaries by Hawkins and Reeve and their collaborators. These volumes may possibly never be bettered.

Although I find historical and architectural information on engine sheds irresistible, the appeal of the engine shed, as far as I am concerned, lies in the locomotives and the associated activities. The present book is a selection of photographs from my own collection and those of Hubert Casserley, Ken Fairey, John Hillmer, David Holmes and, of course, W.A.C. Smith, and is intended to remind the reader of the locomotive shed and the men who worked unstintingly to maintain Britain's railway system. I realise that there are considerable gaps in geographical coverage but I hope that the selectivity will be understood.

The book itself is divided into nine chapters. Chapter 1 shows a selection of sheds, both large and small, from Salisbury to Kipps. Chapter 2 covers scenes inside sheds. Large engine sheds could be cold, dark and slightly disconcerting. They could, however, be transformed by shafts of sunlight penetrating some disintegrating section of the roof. Chapter 3 deals with some of the activities that were carried out to ensure that a locomotive was ready at the right time for its next duty. Chapter 4 shows scenes 'in the yard', a place where the maximum number of engines could be seen, possibly photographed, but certainly have their numbers written down. Railway operation demanded dedication and loyalty from its employees, and Chapter 5 shows some of the men who devoted a considerable part of their lives to locomotives. Chapter 6 concentrates on the locomotives themselves, while Chapter 7 covers some of the duties performed by the engines. Some aspects of the end of the steam locomotive and the sheds are shown in Chapter 8, and an Appendix gives the briefest of glimpses of the contemporary situation.

David Hucknall

Acknowledgements

It gives me very great pleasure to acknowledge those who have contributed to this book. I should like to express my appreciation to Richard Casserley (who provided me with appropriate photographs from his late father's collection), John Hillmer, David Holmes, Ken Fairey and, of course, W.A.C. Smith. I should also like to thank Brian Errington who printed my negatives so competently. Nigel Mussett, a long-standing friend and author of an excellent monograph on the locomotive *Giggleswick*, kindly lent me his colour photographs of Weymouth shed, taken at the very end of steam, and also obtained permission from Mrs Ruby Rutter for me to use her late husband's photograph of 'Patriot' No. 45538 *Giggleswick*.

I am particularly grateful to Peter Alvey who, with great generosity, gave me the photographic collection of his late uncle, George Harrison. Mr Harrison was undoubtedly a photographer of considerable ability. He also corresponded over a number of years with Oliver Bulleid, and observations made by Bulleid on his locomotives are included in some captions.

David Hucknall

Chapter One

A Selection of Sheds

At the end of Platform 4 at Bristol Temple Meads station, trainspotters would gather because of the view it gave of Bath Road shed and yard. Here, beyond 'Castle' Class No. 5084 *Reading Abbey*, the shed can be tantalisingly seen. *(H.G. Usmar/D.J. Hucknall Collection)*

The engine shed at Carstairs probably dated from 1853. It had four roads. By the beginning of the 1930s the depot was 'really in a deplorable condition' (Hawkins and Reeve 1987). Remodelling began in late 1934 and lasted until 1935. Carstairs was a junction of some importance and its shed was involved in a wide range of duties, including passenger work to Glasgow, Edinburgh, Lanark and Peebles. Its importance declined rapidly in the 1960s but it remained long after the removal of steam. Here, A4 Class No. 60024 *Kingfisher*, appropriately cleaned, is seen on Carstairs shed on 19 March 1966, en route from Aberdeen to Nine Elms. In the south, the locomotive worked various railtours. *(W.A.C. Smith)*

Opposite, top: Farnley Junction (shed code 25G until October 1956, then 55C) was a twelve-road straight shed opened in 1882. It was situated within a triangle formed by the main lines (Huddersfield–Wortley South Junction), the Farnley branch and the west–south spur between these two, which also formed part of the depot. This view, looking approximately west across the shed yard, was taken on 20 August 1966, not long before the shed closed. In the yard are Ivatt 4MT No. 43048, 8F No. 48664 and 'Black 5' No. 44845. Behind the tender of the 8F, the 42-bed enginemen's dormitory can be seen. *(David Holmes)*

Opposite, bottom: Salisbury shed stood on slightly raised ground and access was via steps from Cherry Orchard Lane, close to its junction with Churchfield Road. These steps and part of the rear wall of the shed are shown just before demolition in November 1969. Along the rear wall of the shed were offices for the shed foreman and clerks, together with the drivers' lobby. A sign remains, cautioning 'No Admittance except on Business'. *(D.J. Hucknall Collection)*

'Merchant Navy' Class No. 35010 *Blue Star* (rebuilt in January 1957; withdrawn from service in September 1966) is seen standing at the entrance to Exmouth Junction shed. The depot was a twelve–road structure made of concrete. It was a replacement for a much earlier building, 'a vast creaking barn of corrugated iron' (Hawkins and Reeve 1989) that had decayed to the point of collapse. The building shown was opened in 1929. Above the MN's tender can be seen the shed's thirteenth bay, with a raised roof to accommodate an overhead travelling crane. The shed had a saw-tooth roof, with ridges running north to south. The easterly slopes were glazed, while the westerly ones were made of asphalt-covered concrete. *(H.G. Usmar/D.J. Hucknall Collection)*

Opposite, bottom: Eastleigh shed was a large (345ft long; 270ft wide), fifteen-road, straight-through structure with five roof ridges. Originally, it had glazed gable ends and smoke vents that not only ran the length of the ridges but protruded as separate units on the pitches, ventilating wooden smoke ducts inside the shed. In the early days of British Railways, the shed was re-roofed, and corrugated asbestos sheeting replaced the glazing and the pitch roof vents. These modifications are clearly seen in this view of the shed, taken towards the end of its working life. Just two locomotives can be seen outside the shed: Eastleigh Standard Class 4 No. 75059 (transferred from Basingstoke in March 1963) and 'West Country' Class No. 34097 *Holsworthy*. As new, in December 1949, the latter engine was allocated to Ramsgate and remained a 74B locomotive until February 1958, when it was transferred to Bournemouth. In March 1959 it was reassigned to Brighton, moving to Exmouth Junction in late 1960 and, eventually, to Eastleigh. *(H.G. Usmar/D.J. Hucknall Collection)*

The engine shed for Southampton Docks was located in the Old (Eastern) Docks, west of dry docks 1, 2 and 3. Its engines marshalled the wagons and vans that made up the several freight trains booked daily out of the docks. Adams B4 Class 0–4–0T engines were associated with the shed, Nos 81 *Jersey*, 96 *Normandy*, 97 *Brittany* and 176 *Guernsey* constituting the initial allocation. Within eight years, they were joined by Nos 85 *Alderney*, 86 *Havre*, 89 *Trouville*, 90 *Caen*, 93 *St Malo* and 95 *Honfleur*. On 13 September 1936, several B4s were seen in the shed, including No. 93 *St Malo* and, behind the Austin car, No. 89 *Trouville*. The depot was rebuilt in 1954 and closed in 1970. *(H.C. Casserley)*

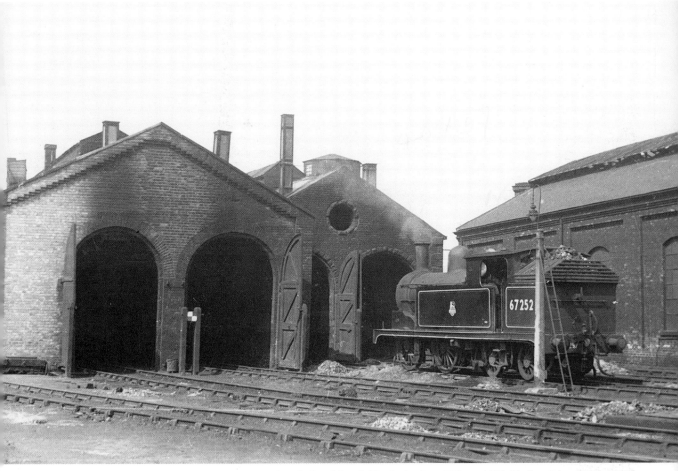

Photographed here are the structures comprising Sunderland South Dock shed on 25 June 1950. To the right of No. 67252 (a Worsdell G5 Class) is the roundhouse, probably opened in September 1874, according to Hoole. In front and to the left of the G5 are two small two-road straight sheds with their large, wooden doors. These sheds were extensively modified by British Railways around 1956 and given flat roofs. Sunderland had nineteen G5s in December 1923. Some twenty-five years later, they continued to play an important role in the workings around Sunderland. It was the introduction of diesel railcars that eventually led to their demise. No. 67252 survived at Sunderland until July 1951 when it was transferred to Gateshead, then Heaton and, finally, Blaydon. It was withdrawn in November 1952. (*H.C. Casserley*)

Opposite, top: On 12 October 1965, V2 Class No. 60816 and A1 Class No. 60145 (formerly *St Mungo*) were seen at Gateshead shed. No. 60816 was a St Margaret's engine at the time and was withdrawn shortly afterwards. No. 60145 entered service at Gateshead in March 1949 and was one of fourteen A1s allocated to the depot. It was, however, stationed at York when this photograph was taken. By January 1966, only Nos 60145 and 60124 of the A1s remained in service. No. 60145 survived until June of that year. (*David Holmes*)

Opposite, bottom: The history of the structures that evolved into Gateshead shed is not clear. Hoole's book indicates that schemes for engine accommodation were discussed by the North Eastern Railway at intervals from September 1854 but it is not clear what was built and when. He does remark, however, 'a diagram of *c.* 1875 shows one large building covering six turntables and their associated radiating roads'. Four of these were in-line and survived until 1956, when two roundhouses were abandoned and the two at the eastern end of the shed were re-roofed and the easternmost turntable replaced by a 70ft example. By 1964, this was removed and the building converted into a straight shed for diesels. Gateshead closed to steam in the latter part of 1965, so the appearance at the shed in September 1967 of 'Castle' Class No. 7029 *Clun Castle* generated considerable local interest. Behind the 'Castle', some of the peculiar mixture of buildings on the shed site can be seen. (*D.J Hucknall*)

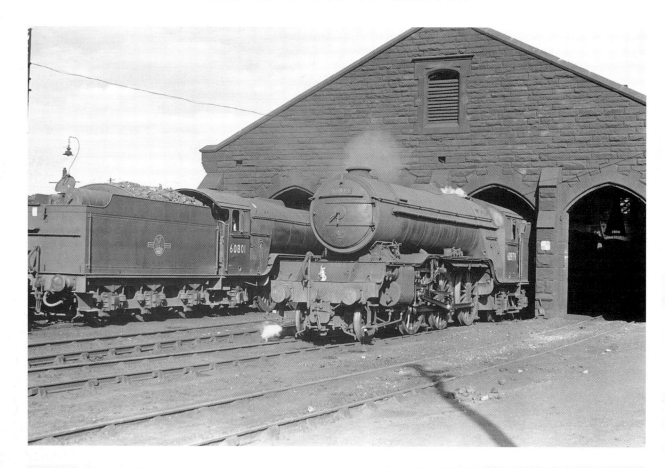

A closer view of the Goods Engine Shed at Worcester on 5 July 1953, taken from the line that led to the Vinegar Works. The centre of attention was 43XX Class 2–6–0 No. 4326, which was standing behind 57XX Class 0–6–0T No. 3607, a long-time Worcester engine. One of the shed staff looked towards the photographer over a shunter's truck (these were provided as transport for the shunters in busy goods yards) on the Gas Works branch. *(J.C. Hillmer)*

Opposite, top: In his monograph on North Eastern locomotive sheds, Hoole gave relatively little detail on the structures at Tweedmouth, except to indicate that no date for the three-road straight shed could be confirmed. It had, however, been re-roofed in 1881. This photograph, taken in the early evening of 9 July 1961, shows the stone straight shed. Standing in the yard are V2 Class locomotives Nos 60801 and 60979. Tweedmouth's allocation of V2s increased from one (No. 3659, later 60932) in 1947 to six in 1954 and nine in 1961. No. 60801 was allocated to the shed from December 1952 to May 1953 and returned in 1955. No. 60979 may have been a visitor from Gateshead. North Eastern V2s worked regularly in Scotland, mostly on express goods services from Newcastle to Edinburgh. *(David Holmes)*

Opposite, bottom: Worcester depot consisted of two sheds – the Passenger Engine Shed and the Goods Engine Shed. The latter is seen in this view taken in the shed yard on 5 July 1953. On the extreme right is the line running to Foregate Street and, eventually, Hereford. The line falling steeply to the immediate left of the shed led to Worcester Gas Works. The engine sheds were situated inside a triangle formed by Tunnel Junction to the north (behind the photographer), Shrub Hill Junction to the south (out of the picture to the left) and Rainbow Hill Junction to the west. A report on the shed situation at Worcester in early 1958 by the British Transport Commission British Railways Western Region Shed Analysis Committee concluded that the layout and facilities offered for the servicing and disposal of its allocation of eighty-five engines were very poor. Although the building has now gone, in July 1999 I photographed Tunnel Junction Signal-box's banner repeater of the Down Droitwich starter from the concrete floor, which is all that remains of the Goods Engine Shed. *(J.C. Hillmer)*

After it was closed to steam, Penzance shed at Long Rock was being used to service diesel locomotives. Seen here on Monday 30 March 1964, Class A1A-A1A 'Warship' diesel-hydraulic locomotive No. D604 *Cossack*, built by the North British Locomotive Company, stands outside the former repair shop. To the right, the former boiler- and pump-houses can be seen. The five A1A-A1A 'Warships' were not successful. They were withdrawn from December 1967 and stored at Laira depot. British Railways considered them life-expired after a mere ten years. *(D.J. Hucknall)*

Opposite, top: This is the former S & DJR shed and yard at Bath on 15 September 1951. The shed, dating from 1874, consisted initially of a two-road timber shed. An identical two-road extension was added three years later. The overall shed was approximately 300ft long and 60ft wide. Each track had a pit that ran the length of the shed. In this view, 'Black 5' No. 45263, then a Leicester engine, and one of Bath's 3P 4–4–0s, No. 40700, stand in the yard. The coaling stage is on the right. Excursion trains from the north would enter Bath (Green Park) station and those for the S & D would be taken forward to Bournemouth. The original train engine would reverse out of the station and proceed to the turntable before running back onto the shed for servicing. *(H.C. Casserley)*

Opposite, bottom: The original South Eastern Railway shed at Reading opened in 1852 and closed in 1875. It was replaced by the then South Eastern & Chatham Railway. Wear and tear meant that in the 1950s the gable ends of the shed had to be rebuilt and the structure re-roofed in the then-ubiquitous corrugated asbestos sheeting. Locomotives serving the Reading–Redhill–Tonbridge route were stabled and serviced at Reading South shed, and in this view taken on 8 February 1960 the 'N' Class locomotives Nos 31830 and 31867 were carrying route discs indicating their involvement in Reading via East Croydon and Redhill (also Tonbridge and Reading) services. Although No. 31867 was a Redhill engine at the time, No. 31830 was allocated to 72A. The 'Schools' V Class No. 30903 *Charterhouse* was a 70C (Guildford) engine. Reading South was a sub-shed of Guildford. *(H.G. Usmar/D.J. Hucknall Collection)*

Two 'Black 5s' are shown at the entrance to Oban shed on 19 April 1952. One of them, No. 44923, was a St Rollox engine at the time. Relatively few locomotives (five by the end of 1947) were allocated to Oban, and apparently the long and costly transport of locomotive coal to the depot made the line a suitable and early candidate for dieselisation. The shed closed in July 1962, when its locomotives were transferred to Perth. *(W.A.C. Smith)*

Opposite, top: Described as 'hidden and remote, in the midst of a confusion of lines and yards' (Hawkins and Reeve 1987), Yoker shed came into operation around March 1907, just prior to the opening of Rothesay Dock in August of the same year. Rothesay Dock was to provide a significant amount of work for Yoker shed over the years. The shed was designated an outstation of Dawsholm and remained a sub-shed throughout LMS days. In 1949 it was given the code 65G with an allocation of twelve engines (a 2F 0–6–0, five 3F 0–6–0Ts, four 2F 0–6–0Ts and two 0–4–0STs). By 1950 locomotive numbers had increased to thirteen and included McIntosh 782 Class 3F goods tank No. 56250, which is shown here at Yoker together with No. 56344 on 20 April 1952. *(H.C. Casserley)*

Opposite, bottom: The shed at Princes Pier, Greenock, was built in 1869 by the Glasgow and South Western Railway to serve its line and ferry terminal there. A feature of the shed was the roof vents, to which unusual extensions were fitted in 1952 after years of subjecting nearby residents to smoke and fumes. In this photograph, taken on 1 August 1953, former Caledonian Railway 4–4–0 No. 54453 stands by the coaling stage while Fairburn 2–6–4T No. 42691 takes water. *(W.A.C. Smith)*

The North British Railway acquired the Monkland and Kirkintilloch Railway, and with it an engine shed that became Kipps locomotive depot. It had three roads and a 50ft turntable. In later years, Kipps received a concrete mechanical coaling stage, which might have been the envy of some larger depots. Kipps (65E) serviced a modest allocation of mainly shunting and freight locomotives, 'employed on the daily routine of getting coal from the mines to the iron works and the subsequent iron and steel to the customers' (J. Howie). There was also a tendency for the shed to gather obsolete or worn-out locomotives that eked out their days before withdrawal. Here, Class Y9 0–4–0ST No. 68114 (a Holmes design for the NBR introduced in 1882 and permanently attached to a wooden tender) is seen on 30 April 1960. The tender was a feature of several Y9s and allowed them to be outstationed in locations where coal might not be conveniently available. Curiously, No. 68114 retained its 62B (Dundee Tay Bridge) shed-plate although it had been transferred to Dawsholm (65D) in April 1958. It moved to Kipps in May 1959. *(W.A.C. Smith)*

Opposite, top: This view of the shed and yard at Fort William was taken on 5 September 1954. In the yard were J36s Nos 65300 and 65313 (both Fort William engines), together with an unidentified 'Black 5'. The shed was opened in 1894 during the time of the North British Railway's move into the West Highlands. It was a two-road shed built of brick. The single-pitch roof had very unusual tapering smoke vents. It closed in December 1962. *(W.A.C. Smith)*

Opposite, bottom: Four Y9 Class 0–4–0Ts (formerly North British Railway Class G) stand in the former St Margaret's Works and Locomotive Depot on 20 June 1937. The depot stood adjacent to Clockmill Road, on the opposite side of the main line from the straight shed. By this time, the roof of the original roundhouse had gone and engines Nos 9042, 10095 and 9010, with their three-link couplings and metal-covered wooden buffers, were clearly visible. The Class Gs were built from 1882 to 1899 for dock and other light shunting duties. At the Grouping, the LNER had acquired thirty-five examples, of which twelve were at St Margaret's and used on Leith Docks, the sidings at Granton and the South Leith branch. They gave good service, and as late as 1953 thirty-three of the class remained. Of the locomotives here, 10095 was withdrawn in March 1953, 9010 in 1955 and 9042 in 1957. *(H.C. Casserley)*

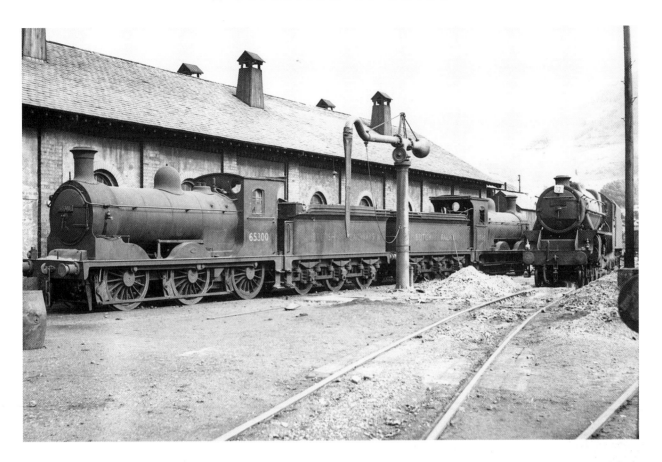

Traffic generated by Grangemouth Docks was of considerable importance to the Caledonian Railway. In 1897 a new shed was built at 'Fouldubs'. It was a six-road straight shed with a single-road repair shop (to the lower left of the pylon in the picture). 'Fouldubs' lay in the fork of the Grangemouth line and the Grahamstown branch. In this photograph, J37 Class No. 64610 and BR Standard Class 3 No. 76100 (allocated to Grangemouth in October 1964) stand outside the shed together with diesel shunters, other J37s and a 'Black 5'. *(D.J. Hucknall)*

Opposite, bottom: The two-road engine shed at Hawick was built by the North British Railway. It was constructed of stone with arched, gated entrances and a steeply pitched roof. Sometime in the mid-1950s, the shed was significantly altered. The original roof was removed and the entrance opened to include both roads. Several courses of brickwork were added to reduce the pitch of the roof and the gable ends were appropriately bricked. In this view, taken on 2 September 1960, the modified shed is clearly seen. Two very grimy engines, Reid C16 4–4–2T No. 67489 and J35 No. 64494, were standing close to the shed entrance. A real disadvantage for the shed was the position of its turntable. It was located on the track leading to the coaling stage. If the turntable was out of action, engines could not reach the stage. The turntable was also too small to accommodate large engines, which had to go to Riccarton Junction to be turned. *(W.A.C. Smith)*

A very unusual view of the former Highland Railway engine shed at Inverness, taken on 19 July 1931 from the buffer beam on No. 15010, a David Jones-designed 4–4–0T passenger tank engine. In the background, a variety of surprisingly grubby engines can be seen. By this date, the free-standing smoke vents and the shed doors, which were fitted to the original structure, had been removed. Some thirty year later, most of the depot's steam locomotives had been withdrawn or transferred, and by August 1962 even its stored locomotives had been moved to Perth. As for the shed, a supermarket now covers the site. As a reminder, however, of the past, a circle of stones is set into the surface of the car park marking the position of the former turntable. *(H.C. Casserley)*

BR Standard Class 2 No. 78050 went, as new, to Motherwell shed (66B). Here it is at the north end of 66B on 4 August 1956. Motherwell shed opened in March 1866. It was concerned with freight duties and 'soldiered on' with steam until May 1967, the date that marked the end of Scottish steam. The building remained in use as a signing-on point for the crews of diesel locomotives, and that would normally be the end of the story. However, a report in the June 1999 issue of the *Journal of the Engine Shed Society* stated, 'By far the most pleasant surprise in Scotland these days is to be found at Motherwell where the entire stone-built 8-road Caledonian Railway steam shed is not only in everyday use but actually increasing in importance as EWS' main traction depot north of the Border'. *(W.A.C. Smith)*

Opposite, top: The engine shed at Riccarton Junction was a sub-shed of Hawick. It was a lean-to structure attached to a coaling stage and could accommodate two engines. It is shown here on 28 April 1952. Outside the shed was J35 No. 64509, a Hawick engine, which remained as a 64G engine until its withdrawal in October 1959. One Riccarton Junction locomotive (the pilot engine) was in constant use and manned on a three-shift basis. Its duties involved assisting trains up the bank from Newcastleton to Whitrope, shunting in the goods yard at Riccarton and dealing with the daily (Monday–Saturday) morning goods down the Reedsmouth branch, returning at about 1 p.m. The other Riccarton engine worked the 7.12 a.m. passenger train to Carlisle and returned with a goods train at lunchtime. When the pilot engine was occupied, an engine and crew from Hawick were sent for banking duties. *(H.C. Casserley)*

Opposite, bottom: The west end of Thornton Junction shed is shown on 25 March 1961. On the left stands J36 No. 65261, with its tender fitted with a cab for the cooler days in the east of Scotland. In front of the J36 is B1 Class No. 61330, while on the right is J83 0–6–0T No. 68459. Built by the LNER and opened in 1933, the shed shown replaced an older, overcrowded structure opened in 1896 by the North British Railway. The LNER shed had six through roads and a two-road repair shop equipped with a wheel-drop, lifting and machining facilities. It also had the pagoda-like tops to the smoke outlets, which I found quite charming. *(W.A.C. Smith)*

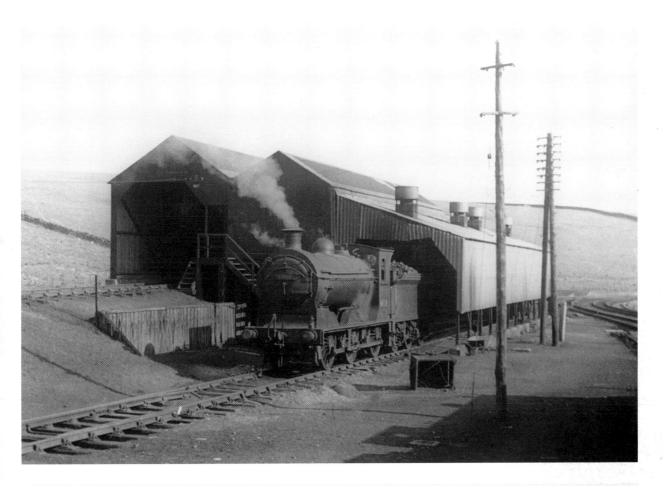

Ayr shed opened around 1878. It was built in red sandstone and had two gables, each covering three roads. This view, taken on 31 March 1961, shows part of the original structure and Hughes/Fowler 'Crab' 2–6–0 No. 42910. Adjacent to the locomotive is one of the extensions to the west gable. Extensions at both the north and south ends of the shed were added around 1959 on the arrival of six-car diesel multiple units, leaving three roads on the eastern part of the shed for steam locomotives. No. 42910 was transferred to Ayr from Hurlford in June 1954 and, apart from a brief return to Hurlford, it remained an Ayr engine at least up to the time of this photograph. The 'Crabs' were frequently used on coal trains from the Ayrshire coalfields and were thoroughly recorded in the excellent photographs of Derek Cross. (*D.J. Hucknall Collection*)

Chapter Two

Inside

George Harrison produced some fine night-time photographs using only the available
light. Here, rebuilt 'Battle of Britain' Class No. 34056 *Croydon* stands in Salisbury shed
in 1966. The locomotive retained its name plates until March the following year.
They are now held by the RAF Museum at Cosford. No. 34056 was withdrawn on
7 May 1967, from Salisbury mpd. It continued to be stored there until August 1967
before being moved to Cashmore's at Newport and scrapped the following month.
(George Harrison/D.J. Hucknall Collection)

Light from the shed entrance reflected off the front end of 'West Country' Class No. 34100 *Appledore* inside Salisbury shed on an August day in 1966. The locomotive was allocated to Ramsgate mpd in December 1949 and remained one of its locomotives until February 1958, when it was transferred to Stewarts Lane. It emerged from rebuilding in September 1960 and was withdrawn from Salisbury in July 1966. In the background, part of a diesel multiple unit can be seen. In the mid-1960s, dmus handled most of the Salisbury local services to the west of the city. *(George Harrison/ D.J. Hucknall Collection)*

Opposite: Creditably clean 'West Country' Class No. 34013 *Okehampton* was photographed inside Salisbury shed. The date was probably sometime in 1966. At the time, Salisbury shed had sufficient staff for the shedmaster, Mr Claud Dare, to allocate men to locomotive cleaning. No. 34013 survived until the end of steam on the Southern Region, working the 17.13 Weymouth–Waterloo on 7 July 1967. *(George Harrison/D.J. Hucknall Collection)*

'West Country' Class No. 34005 *Barnstaple* was the first of Bulleid's Light Pacifics to be rebuilt, work starting in June 1957. What emerged was a strikingly handsome locomotive. The rebuilding programme appalled Bulleid, who wrote the following to George Harrison in January 1966: 'Whoever authorised the rebuilding of these engines at the age they were ought to be made to pay the cost instead of the taxpayer. To have so much trouble with heated big-ends and then remove the oil-bath that cured the problem passes comprehension.'

Opposite: A detailed view of the front end of unrebuilt 'West Country' Class No. 34006 *Bude* inside the engine shed at Salisbury. As No. 21C106, *Bude* was built at Brighton Works in 1945, part of a batch numbered 21C101–21C148. The new locomotives were scaled-down versions of the 'Merchant Navy' Class and were intended to have the same route availability as the Class N 2–6–0s. No. 34006 was one of three 'West Country' Class engines (the others being Nos 34004 and 34005) that performed so well in the 1948 Locomotive Exchanges. The men who crewed the Light Pacifics over the years seemed to appreciate Bulleid's efforts on their behalf in their design. Writing to George Harrison, retired driver Reg Hayman (72A) said, 'Later, when the "West Country" Class came to Exmouth Junction, Driver R. Dawe and myself had No. 10, which was named *Sidmouth*, to ourselves, early and late turns of duty on the run Exeter to Ilfracombe, and what a grand and reliable engine to have had, and what a lovely ride. Everyone really admired those engines, what a great pity they were ever taken out of service.' *(George Harrison/D.J. Hucknall Collection)*

The afternoon sun on 29 March 1965 penetrated the interior of the main shed at Dalry Road and illuminated delightfully 'Black 5' No. 44975. In the early 1950s, the locomotive was assigned to Perth. It was transferred to Oban in December 1954 and remained there certainly until the end of 1960, although it seems to have been given to Fort William in the spring of 1961. *(D.J. Hucknall)*

Opposite, top: The Midland Railway's engine shed at Bristol was opened in 1873. It was laid out as a roundhouse with a 42ft turntable. The latter was replaced in 1927 by one of 60ft in diameter. In this photograph, taken on 20 April 1934, 3F 0–6–0 No. 3181 can be seen. The engine is clean, the smoke troughs are in good order and the shed seems to have had high standards of maintenance. No. 3181 was part of Bristol's allocation in 1920, and remained there certainly until the mid-1940s. A decade later, the engine was in Canklow's tender care. It was withdrawn from Sheffield in 1957. *(H.C. Casserley)*

Opposite, bottom: This fine photograph of the inside of Eastfield shed on 2 April 1966 shows former Dalry Road 'Black 5' No. 45477 together with two unidentified locomotives. Of these two locomotives, the tender of the leading engine is overfilled with the most appalling-looking coal. *(W.A.C. Smith)*

The former Highland Railway Drummond 4–4–0 (one of the 'Small Bens') No. 54398 *Ben Alder* is shown in the shed at Boat of Garten. The locomotive, a long-time resident at Wick, was withdrawn in February 1953 and stored at Boat of Garten awaiting preservation. It was to have been the sixth Scottish locomotive (CR No. 123, NBR No. 256, GNSR No. 49, GSWR No. 9 and the Jones 'Goods' being the others) to be preserved, but in 1966, despite many assurances to the contrary given by the British Railways Board and the British Transport Commission, it was cut up. *(D.J. Hucknall Collection)*

Opposite: A group of railway enthusiasts strolled past J72 Class No. 69001 in the roofless Springhead shed (53C), Hull, on 24 August 1952. Springhead was located approximately 3 miles to the west of Hull and was built by the Hull and Barnsley Railway around 1885. By 1906 the shed had eight through roads, but its facilities were fairly basic. After Nationalisation the depot's allocation began to be run down. The shed buildings gradually lost their roof and the locomotives were transferred to Dairycoats on 30 November 1958. By 15 December 1958, it was officially closed to steam. In a railway auction in October 2004, a 53C shed plate realised £880. *(J.C. Hillmer)*

The absurdity of the prolonged rebuilding programme for the Bulleid Light Pacifics is well illustrated with the example of 'West Country' No. 34104 *Bere Alston*, seen here inside Salisbury shed with No. 34095 *Brentor*. No. 34104 was completed at Eastleigh Works on 11 May 1961, completing the rebuilding programme for selected Bulleid Pacifics. It was withdrawn from service in June 1967 as, effectively, a six-year-old locomotive. Bulleid's comment at the beginning of 1966 to George Harrison was that whoever authorised the rebuilding programme for his Pacifics at the age they were, should be made to pay the cost. He further wrote, 'These I think are symptoms of the illness – Nationalisation. The engine drivers do not seem to have any doubt about their regard for the original layout.' *(George Harrison/D.J. Hucknall Collection)*

Opposite: An exceptional photograph of BR Standard Class 4 2–6–0 No. 76067 taken inside Salisbury shed. No. 76067 was completed in August 1956 and allocated to Eastleigh. From there it would have worked on Brighton–Bournemouth through trains, to and from Salisbury with Portsmouth–Cardiff trains, and over the Didcot, Newbury and Southampton line. The locomotive was transferred to Salisbury in 1960 and to Bournemouth in April 1967. It survived until the end of steam on the Southern Region. *(George Harrison/D.J.Hucknall Collection)*

Deeley 4P three-cylinder Compound No. 1007 was photographed inside Cricklewood shed on 7 July 1937. Cricklewood shed consisted of two roundhouses, the first opened in 1882, while the other (No. 2 shed) came into operation in 1893. From the point of view of locomotive servicing, it must have been considerably more convenient and reassuring to work in a roundhouse compared to a straight shed. The effectiveness of the suspended gas lamp is debatable if work had to be carried out on an engine at night. (H.C. Casserley)

This view of the interior of Salisbury shed looking towards the back wall, sometime in 1966, shows rebuilt 'West Country' No. 34100 (formerly *Appledore*) in the foreground and 'Warship' diesel No. D870 *Zulu* towards the rear. Light streams through the roof and shows clearly the junction of the asbestos pitches of the British Railways re-roofing at the front of the shed and the original gables at the rear. The original gable-end glazing is very apparent behind the diesel. *(George Harrison/D.J. Hucknall Collection)*

Opposite, bottom: The North Eastern Railway, needing to enlarge Paragon Street station in Hull, had to remove two engine sheds. The new shed at Botanic Gardens opened in 1901. To house the locomotives, two 50ft turntables each served twenty-four radiating roads. Taken on 21 June 1931, this photograph shows five roads radiating from one of the turntables. The locomotive on the left is a G5 Class, No. 2088, which was allocated to Botanic Gardens in 1928. The centre locomotive, No. 957, was an X2 Class 2–2–4T, a former NER 'BTP' Class 0–4–4T from 1874, rebuilt in 1903 for hauling the inspection saloon of the Hull District Superintendent. From the date of its rebuilding to its withdrawal in April 1937, except for the winter of 1931/32, No. 957 spent its working life at Botanic Gardens. *(H.C. Casserley)*

Heaton shed on 11 June 1965 contained B1 Class No. 61199 (of Blaydon, 52C) and J27 Class 0–6–0s Nos 65789, 65819 and 65858. Originally classified by the North Eastern Railway as P3s, No. 65789 (as No. 938 in 1923) had been built in 1906; No. 65819 (No. 1029) and No. 65858 (No. 1230) were of 1908 vintage. I have always liked O.S. Nock's description of the class: 'They were hard-slogging, honest-to-goodness "colliers", and little else.' Withdrawal began in March 1959, but by June 1966 there were still thirty-six of the class hard at work, most of them involved in moving coal in south Northumberland and County Durham. *(David Holmes)*

Sunlight filtering through the roof of St Margaret's shed illuminated the buffer beam of A3 Class No. 60100 *Spearmint* on 20 March 1965, a few weeks before the engine was withdrawn from service. The locomotive (as No. 2796) entered service in May 1930 from Haymarket shed. Throughout its working life it was allocated to Scottish sheds, having a long and distinguished association with Haymarket (May 1930 to April 1937; March to July 1938; December 1940 to January 1963). While at Haymarket, *Spearmint* began a long association with Norman McKillop who, under his pen-name Toram Beg, entertained countless railway enthusiasts with tales of the locomotive. *(D.J. Hucknall)*

Opposite, bottom: Another example of the late George Harrison's excellent photographs shows 'West Country' Class No. 34026 *Yes Tor* (72A, May 1949 to April 1951; 70A, April 1951 to January 1958; Ramsgate, February to June 1958 (rebuilding, February/March 1958); 73A, June 1958 to November 1960) in the shed at Salisbury. It had been allocated to Salisbury since November 1960. Salisbury appeared to be a fairly well-lit shed, with electric lights down each road. Hoole (1972), however, pointed out the difficulties of working on a locomotive at night in some circumstances: '. . . if work had to be done it often had to be carried out by the flickering light of a naked-flame paraffin lamp with its smoking flame going this way and that in the draughts.' *(George Harrison/D.J. Hucknall Collection)*

From the point of view of cleanliness, conditions inside a working steam locomotive shed were considered inappropriate for diesel locomotives, and separation of the two forms of traction was recommended. This was apparently not recognised at Salisbury mpd when this photograph was taken of 'Warship' Class No. D870 *Zulu*. From 1964 until 1971, the 'Warships' were the principal locomotives on the Waterloo–Exeter services.

On 10 March 1964, trial running and crew training began on the Exeter–Salisbury line with Type 4 'Warship' Class locomotive No. D827 *Kelly*. At the beginning of June that year, No. D829 *Magpie* arrived at Salisbury for crew training involving three return trips daily to Basingstoke. Later in the year, *The Railway Observer* (December 1964) reported, 'It is depressing to record little or no improvement in time-keeping on the West of England services to and from Waterloo. Failure of "Warship" diesels are too frequent and the number of times that steam has replaced diesel traction is too often to record.' Here, one of the much-maligned 'Warship' Type 4s is seen inside Salisbury shed sometime in 1965. *(George Harrison/D.J. Hucknall Collection)*

Throughout the 1950s, B1 Class No. 61221 *Sir Alexander Erskine-Hill* was based at Haymarket shed and, faintly on the buffer beam, this fact can still be seen. The locomotive is shown here inside the shed at Dundee Tay Bridge, a subsequent allocation, on 6 March 1965. *(D.J. Hucknall)*

Old Oak Common was a very large shed, the building containing four turntables, each serving twenty-five stabling roads. Here, two 9Fs and two 57XX Class 0–6–0PTs are seen around one of the turntables. The two pannier tanks had a long association with Old Oak Common, being on the allocation in 1947, although No. 8770 moved to Slough in 1960. The identifiable 9F, No. 92240, spent a relatively short time as an Old Oak engine (November 1958 to September 1960). It is now preserved. (*H.G. Usmar/D.J. Hucknall*)

Chapter Three

Preparation/Disposal

Ready for the off, 'West Country' Class No. 34100 (formerly *Appledore*) stands at the front of Salisbury shed, its safety valves lightly blowing. *(George Harrison/D.J. Hucknall Collection)*

Unrebuilt 'Battle of Britain' Class No. 34057 *Biggin Hill* gleams as it stands inside Salisbury shed. Nearby is a pair of steps to reach the upper parts of the locomotive. The shed floor is commendably clean and a wheelbarrow is nearby. George Harrison, who corresponded with Oliver Bulleid for a few years, received a letter from him in July 1966, concerning a letter Mr Harrison had sent to the press. In his letter, Bulleid remarked, 'I am glad you called the paper's readers' attention to the way the Sarum men kept the engines clean. It shows the latent goodwill of the Staff had the Management known how to appeal to it.' *(George Harrison/D.J. Hucknall Collection)*

A delightful view of rebuilt 'Battle of Britain' Class No. 34052 (formerly *Lord Dowding*) at Salisbury shed, shown during preparation for one of its last duties. The locomotive was standing close to one of the water columns and one of the crew is on the running-plate topping up the mechanical lubricators. On the ground, by the pile of ashes, two small oilcans had been left. *(George Harrison/D.J. Hucknall Collection)*

With clean topsides at least, 'Battle of Britain' Class No. 34052 (formerly *Lord Dowding*) is seen taking water at Salisbury shed in May 1967, prior to its next duty, the 'Feltham Goods'. In the last days of Southern steam, No. 34052 was quite active. On 5 July 1967 it worked the 19.06 Portsmouth–Cardiff goods. On 7 July it was seen on the Basingstoke–Eastleigh, which then worked onwards as the 19.45 to Bournemouth. *(George Harrison/D.J. Hucknall Collection)*

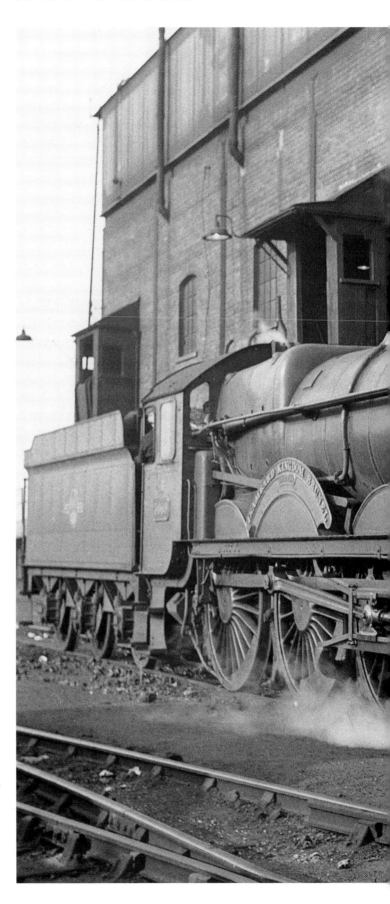

Plymouth Laira's 'Castle' Class No. 5069 *Isambard Kingdom Brunel* on duty no. 212, according to the train reporting number, seen by the coaling stage at Bristol Bath Road shed. The coaling stage was 90ft long and had three coal tips. Typically, the inner floor of the coaler was steel-plated and the coaling tubs, with their metal wheels, were manhandled across to the tips and the coal shot into the locomotive's bunker. *(H.G. Usmar/D.J. Hucknall Collection)*

'V2' Class 2–6–2 No. 60931 stands by the side of one of the three water columns in the yard of the main shed at St Margaret's in February 1965. In the background, across the railway lines, is part of the stone structure on Clockmill Road, which had once been part of the old St Margaret's Works and Locomotive Depot. The water column was typical of the North British Railway and was fitted with a stove to prevent the water freezing in the winter. *(D.J. Hucknall)*

Opposite, top: Standing under New England shed's watering gantry on 18 February 1962 were King's Cross's well-cared-for A4 No. 60017 *Silver Fox* and New England V2 No. 60803. Despite the obvious advantages of having a locomotive-watering system capable of delivering at least 1,000 gallons per minute from each outlet, only York, King's Cross Top Shed and New England had such structures. The King's Cross system was installed in 1952 and that at New England shortly afterwards. In June 1963, on the closure of Top Shed, No. 60017 was one of eleven A4s redeployed to New England. A short time afterwards, it was taken out of service. *(K.C.H. Fairey)*

Opposite, bottom: 'Black 5' No. 45156 *Ayrshire Yeomanry* was taking water at Farnley Junction shed on 27 November 1960. By this time, it was allocated to Newton Heath. Until its transfer in April 1957, No. 45156 had been based at St Rollox, together with its sisters Nos 45154, 45157 and 45158. The four were the only named 'Black 5s' and, with their distinctive name-plates with their regimental badges, they were rare indeed in England. The smokebox number-plate was also unusual. The numbers are of the LMS 1936 pattern which, although used in 1936/37, were still to be found on some locomotives (for example, No. 45477) until the 1960s. *(David Holmes)*

Former Caledonian Railway Class 2F 0–6–0T No. 56159 trundled off the ash pits at Polmadie depot on 12 April 1958. Coupled to the 0–6–0T was Standard 2–6–4T No. 80058. The latter locomotive was allocated to Polmadie in January 1955 and was withdrawn from the same shed in July 1966. *(W.A.C. Smith)*

Pickersgill 113 (3/3P) Class 4–4–0 No. 54495 (Helmsdale, 60C) heads a line of engines on the disposal road leading past the coaling stage at St Rollox/Balornock shed. The date was 25 April 1953. Because of the inadequacy of the existing arrangements at the Caledonian Railway's running sheds at Buchanan Street and St Rollox, new facilities at Balornock came into use on 13 November 1916. According to Hawkins and Reeve (1987), the name 'Balornock' can be regarded as a CR/LMSR term and 'St Rollox' (although the shed was some distance from the Works), a British Railways term. St Rollox/Balornock dealt with a range of duties to Perth and the North. The shed closed from 7 November 1966. *(W.A.C. Smith)*

At the Restalrig Road South end of St Margaret's shed were the fire-cleaning roads. Here, the locomotive ashpan could be raked into the pits, or ash and clinker could be scooped out of the firebox and thrown on to the ground to be later doused with water and shovelled into wagons waiting in the gully. This was an extremely unpleasant task for the engineman involved, as can be imagined from this photograph showing an A3 Class locomotive wreathed in steam and fumes from the operation. *(D.J. Hucknall)*

'Royal Scot' Class No. 46118 *Royal Welch Fusilier* was allocated briefly to Derby (17 June to 26 August 1961). During that period it was seen in the dirt and clutter of the yard at Kingmoor shed. The date was 7 August 1961. The job of engine disposal had been left unfinished, the buffer beam being covered with smokebox char. Until January 1960, No. 46118 had always been associated with the West Coast Main Line, but in that month it began a short association with the Midland Main Line when it was added to Nottingham's stock. *(D.J. Hucknall)*

Opposite, top: With cylinder cocks open, A4 Class No. 60027 *Merlin* stood by the coaling stage at St Margaret's on 27 March 1965. It looked particularly run-down and neglected, a shadow of the locomotive that had been one of a superb group handling expresses on the East Coast Main Line. The locomotive entered service in March 1937 as LNER No. 4486 at Haymarket shed. It remained on that shed's allocation until May 1962, when it was transferred to St Rollox shed. It was reported at the time that, with few exceptions, the St Rollox men did not like the A4s. In September 1964 No. 60027 went to St Margaret's, where it soldiered on until withdrawal from service in September 1965. *(D.J. Hucknall)*

Opposite, bottom: A4 Class No. 60026 *Miles Beevor*, looking grubby and run-down, stands by the coaling stage at St Margaret's on a damp Saturday afternoon in February 1965. When new in February 1937, as No. 4485 *Kestrel*, the locomotive was allocated to Haymarket. It was renamed *Miles Beevor* in November 1947. May 1951 saw the engine re-allocated to King's Cross Top Shed for the third time. It remained there until that shed closed, when it went to New England for further duties. In October 1963 it was one of several of the class sent to Scotland. No. 60026 entered service again in the summer of 1964 on the Glasgow–Edinburgh service. It was withdrawn nine months after this photograph was taken. *(D.J. Hucknall)*

In the late 1920s and early 1930s, 4P Compounds were the largest engines available at Bristol LMS shed to work the Birmingham expresses. 'Black 5s' and 'Jubilees' were allocated to the depot in the 1930s and then assumed these duties. Here, Saltley (21A) 5P5F No. 5038 is standing alongside the original coaling stage at Bristol on 27 May 1935. Typical of these early Class 5s, No. 5038 had a domeless boiler. In the background, the parapet of the bridge carrying Barrow Road over the shed yard can be seen. The old coaler was replaced around 1938/39 with a Type 2 LMS coaling plant. *(H.C. Casserley)*

Opposite, top: J37 No. 64617 stood in front of the engine shed at Alloa on 3 October 1959. The two-road shed was built by the North British Railway and opened in 1885 (Hooper, *LNER Sheds in Camera*, 1984). The entrance had large, hinged wooden doors. An unidentified J36 was also present. The structure above both locomotives is part of the coaling system. Wheeled hoppers (seen between the engines) were filled with coal and raised above the tender or hopper using a motorised hoist (from which a chain was dangling). When in position, the hopper door would be unlatched, allowing coal to be discharged. *(W.A.C. Smith)*

Opposite, bottom: Overcoaled 'Battle of Britain' Class No. 34089 *602 Squadron* is seen on the preparation road leading to the coaling stage at Salisbury. When new, the locomotive was assigned to Ramsgate shed. It became a Salisbury engine in September 1963 and, even close to the end of steam, it retained its name-plates and squadron crests. It was in use on 7 July 1967, the last day of steam working on the Southern Region, working a Waterloo–Southampton East Docks train. It remained in store at Salisbury until March 1968, when it was removed to Cashmore's in Newport. *(George Harrison/ D.J. Hucknall Collection)*

'Patriot' Class No. 45508 was seen close to the coaler at its home shed, Preston, on 26 April 1949. One of the locomotive's crew is trimming the coal on the tender, while the other one appears to be looking closely at the exhaust from the right-hand injector. The coaler was situated to the south-west of the main shed as part of the preparation/disposal area that included the ash plant, water columns and turntable. No. 45508 was never given a name. It was transferred from Preston to Carlisle Upperby in September 1951. It returned to Preston's allocation briefly in November 1959. *(H.C. Casserley)*

Opposite, top: Looking towards the old 'tank over' coal stage at Farnley Junction shed from a vantage point near the newer coaling plant on 10 March 1964, 'Jubilee' Class No. 45581 *Bihar and Orissa* was seen moving away from the coaler. According to Hawkins and Reeve (1981), the newer coal plant, together with a new ash plant, was installed at Farnley Junction shed because of the exceedingly long disposal times that were recorded at the shed. Six hours to coal, water and turn an engine had not been unusual. *(David Holmes)*

Opposite, bottom: 'Black 5' No. 45122, probably an Inverness-based locomotive at the time, in ex-Works condition, stands by the rather dilapidated coaling stage at Balornock on 19 June 1949. Locomotives fresh from St Rollox Works were often run in by allowing the shed to use them for various duties. *(H.C. Casserley)*

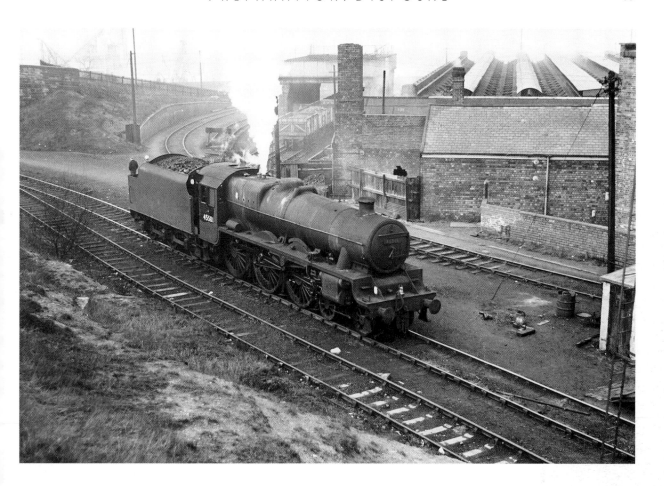

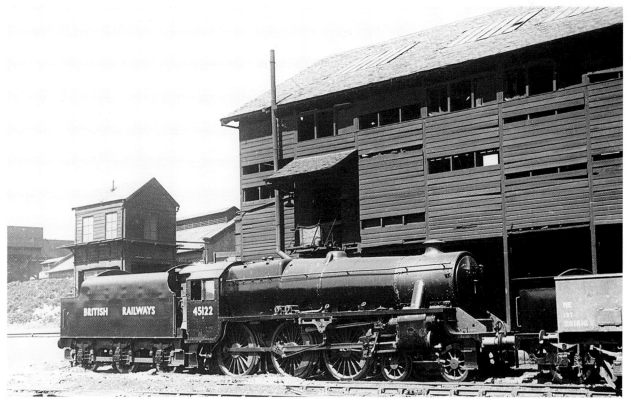

A3 Class No. 60073 *St Gatien* was seen near the coaling stage at Heaton Junction on the afternoon of 27 April 1958. The single-sided coaling stage was fitted with three discharge chutes. *St Gatien* was a Heaton engine for many years (May 1946 to June 1963). In the early 1950s, a Heaton locomotive would work a daily Newcastle–Bournemouth train that used the former Great Central line at Doncaster and travelled through Rotherham towards Nottingham and the South. As a boy, it gave me great pleasure to see one of Heaton's A3s (Nos 60069/70/73/77/80 and 60088) pass through Parkgate and Aldwarke station at about 11.30 in the morning in the summer, returning about 4.30 in the afternoon. *(David Holmes)*

Opposite, top: The driver of 'Coronation' Class No. 6224 *Princess Alexandra* was paying close attention to the progress of coaling at Polmadie on 27 August 1945. The locomotive was in plain black livery and, as would be expected at the end of the war, a little work-stained. When built at Crewe in 1937, No. 6224 was allocated to Camden. It was transferred to Polmadie's stock in December 1939 and remained one of its locomotives until it was withdrawn from service. *(H.C. Casserley)*

Opposite, bottom: A very grimy 'Jubilee' Class No. 5730 *Ocean* (12A, 1948–9) is seen at Polmadie depot on 27 October 1945. During disposal the job of smokebox cleaning had not been satisfactorily finished, with char remaining on the buffer beam and under the door. The coaler shown in the photograph had been built in the 1920s to replace a 'coaling station' consisting of a ramp and a shelter. Further modernisation of Polmadie depot eventually took place in the late 1940s. A new coaling plant, having a segregated bunker holding three grades of locomotive coal and a capacity of 400 tons, was brought into use in 1948. *(H.C. Casserley)*

Eastleigh's N15 Class No. 30770 *Sir Prianius* stood near a water column close to the coaling stage at Salisbury on the early afternoon of 16 June 1957. At the time, the shed's allocation consisted of fifty-four locomotives, including eight N15s. In the 1950s the N15s often worked the Salisbury–Exeter passenger services. In the 1930s, however, the 'King Arthur' 4–6–0s were used on the 'Atlantic Coast Express'. An extraordinary run from Salisbury to Waterloo was made in 1936. Driver Alderman with No. 777 *Sir Lamiel* (plus ten coaches) gained 17¼ minutes on a 90-minute allowance. Speeds in the 80s and 90s were achieved between Grateley and Esher. *(David Holmes)*

Coal on the tender of B1 No. 61278 was being trimmed by its fireman at Dundee Tay Bridge (62B) on 6 March 1965. As No. 1278, the locomotive had entered traffic on 19 January 1948 at 62B. It spent its working life there but eventually, in April 1967, it was declared unfit for further service. *(D.J. Hucknall)*

Peppercorn Class A2 No. 60530 *Sayajirao* was standing under the coaler at Dundee Tay Bridge depot on the late morning of 6 March 1965. Allocated briefly to King's Cross Top Shed, No. 60530 next went to New England shed. In January 1950 it went, together with No. 60536, to Haymarket in exchange for Class A2/2s Nos 60504/6. It remained a Haymarket engine until October 1961. In July 1964 it was sent to Tay Bridge shed after a stint at Polmadie. It was withdrawn in November 1966. *(D.J. Hucknall)*

Although its name-plates and RAF insignias had been removed, well-cleaned, unrebuilt 'Battle of Britain' Class No. 34057 (formerly *Biggin Hill*) made a fine picture as it stood by the south side of the coaling stage at Salisbury shed. The coaler was rather a primitive structure in which men shovelled coal into wheeled tubs and then tipped the contents into the locomotive tender. Above the cab of No. 34057, however, a more efficient device can be seen, in the form of a conveyor belt. This was probably introduced when Salisbury had six 'Merchant Navy' Class locomotives (Nos 35004/6–10) in its allocation, as the sides of their tenders were too high to allow tubs to be tipped. George Harrison rarely dated his photographs, but it is likely that this was taken on 9 April 1967 when No. 34057 worked a Special from Salisbury to Southampton via Eastleigh. *(George Harrison/D.J. Hucknall Collection)*

Opposite, bottom: Pickersgill 60 Class 4–6–0 No. 54639 standing at the coaling stage at Hamilton shed on 6 June 1953. The shed had ten roads, but the brick coaling stage with its large overhead water tank caused these to diverge on either side in the shed yard. The Pickersgill 60s were designed for the Caledonian Railway but only six examples were built. After the Grouping, the LMS authorised the production of twenty more and No. 54639 (as No. 14639) was one of the batch produced in 1925/6. It became the last Pickersgill 4–6–0 to remain in service and was withdrawn from Hamilton some six months after this photograph was taken. *(W.A.C. Smith)*

Kingmoor's LMS 4P Compound 4–4–0 No. 1141 was waiting its turn at Polmadie depot's coaler when this photograph was taken on 27 October 1945. Ahead in the queue was a 'Coronation' Class 4–6–2. The Compounds came to Kingmoor in the early summer of 1925. No fewer than twenty arrived for Scottish duties – fifteen (Nos 1135–49) for work on the Caledonian section and five (Nos 1065–9) for work on the Glasgow and South Western lines. Drivers were assigned to each engine, No. 1141 having Driver J. Young initially. Two years later, Polmadie received ten new Compounds and other examples went to a range of Scottish sheds, including Corkerhill, Dalry Road, Perth and Aberdeen. David L. Smith, writing in the *Journal of the Stephenson Locomotive Society* in 1962, described the pre-war work of the Compounds in glowing terms. He went on, 'The start of the 1939 war may be said to mark the end of the great days of the Compounds in Scotland. Years of hard work lay ahead of them. It was done, and usually done well.' *(H.C. Casserley)*

A3 Class No. 60100 *Spearmint* was being turned at St Margaret's on 17 April 1965. In the background, the houses on Restalrig Road South can be seen, while above and behind the brick retaining wall, part of the St Margaret's Loco Men and Women's Institute is visible through No. 60100's exhaust. The actual site of the main shed at St Margaret's is now a car park for nearby office blocks. The stone wall on Restalrig Road South has been opened to provide an entrance to the car park. The wooden door in the wall that provided access to the shed from the rear apparently still remains. *(D.J. Hucknall)*

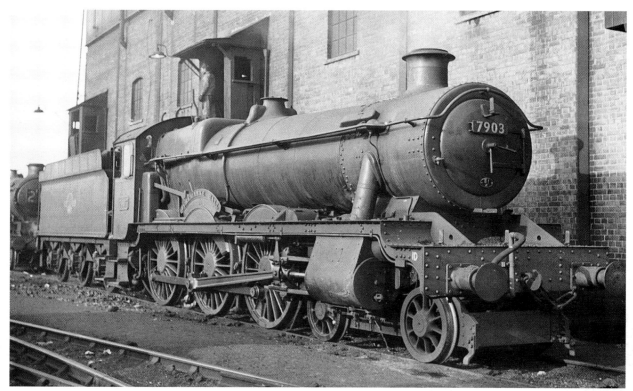

'Modified Hall' No. 7903 *Foremarke Hall* (81A) stands at the coaling stage at Bristol Bath Road. The shed was opened in 1934 and the coaling stage was situated close to the shed on its eastern side. It was a large brick structure with a water tank over the wagon road. It had three coal tips and, apart from the water tank, was very similar to the coaler at Cathays depot, Cardiff (Lyons 1972). *(D.J. Hucknall Collection)*

A superb view of A3 Class No. 60057 *Ormonde* as it stood on the 70ft turntable at Haymarket. The locomotive was built in February 1925 and, at the outset, was a southern area engine (initially allocated to Grantham, moving to King's Cross shed in June 1928 and on to Doncaster in September 1938). It became a Scottish locomotive (at Haymarket) in March 1939, although its allocation changed fairly frequently, its longest stint at Haymarket lasting from April 1943 to December 1961. A name-plate from *Ormonde* was sold at auction in December 2001 for £12,100. *(J. Robertson/Transport Treasury)*

The problem of engine-turning at Grantham, after the turntable had been removed in 1951, was resolved by laying a triangle of lines to the south-west side of the site. Here, on 7 September 1963, A3 Class No. 60112 *St Simon* is standing on one of the lines leading to the turning triangle. In the background, rising above No. 60112, is the shed's mechanical coaler, erected in the late 1930s. Ahead of the locomotive is the large cylindrical tank of the water-softening plant, with a line of disused locomotive tenders close by to act as sludge carriers. These could be seen by the side of the main line at Ranskill, where they were discharged into a 'lagoon'. *(K.C.H. Fairey)*

Under the shear-legs on the south-west side of the 'new' shed at Grantham, O2 Class 2–8–0 No. 63984 was seen on 18 April 1963. In the right background, the locomotive crews' classroom can be seen, where 'mutual improvement' and other appropriate technical training was given. The O2 was built in December 1942 and was withdrawn in November 1963. At the time of this photograph, No. 63984 was a Doncaster engine, and in its last few months before withdrawal it spent time working coal trains from Worksop to Wath Yard. It is possible that on this occasion it had been working a High Dyke iron ore train when some problem occurred, necessitating a visit to Grantham. *(K.C.H. Fairey)*

One of the few unpleasant aspects of the steam locomotive shed from the enthusiast's point of view was the dirt-laden, awful-smelling, brown-black smoke that could roll out of a locomotive chimney during fire preparation. It could pervade a disproportionately large area and really inhibit one's enjoyment. Here, at Grangemouth shed on 29 April 1965, 'Black 5' No. 45443, a St Rollox engine, is shown being prepared for its next duty. No further comment is necessary. *(D.J. Hucknall)*

Chapter Four

In the Yard

'Some members of my Railway Society and I penetrated the weak defences in the dying days of steam.'
This summarised the situation at Eastleigh on 27 May 1967 according to Nigel Mussett, who took this photograph.
In the yard were unrebuilt 'West Country' Class No. 34023 *Blackmore Vale* and Standard Class 4 No. 76069. In the shed at
the time were Class 4 2-6-4 tanks Nos 80133 and 80139 and another Class 4 2–6–0, No. 76031. *(N.J. Mussett)*

Looking remarkably clean and with name-plates intact, rebuilt 'West Country' Class No. 34037 *Clovelly* was seen at Salisbury depot. According to *Trains Illustrated* (March 1960), the Southern Region was offered Gresley A4 Pacifics as an alternative to further rebuilding of the Bulleid Pacifics. The offer was rejected. The rebuilt Bulleids had much support from railwaymen. In a letter to George Harrison, retired Driver Jeffery from 72A said that he could not endorse the view that the unrebuilt locomotives were better than the rebuilt version. Of the rebuilt engines he remarked, 'The screw reverser in one go did away with almost all the trouble as the new gear was almost 100% perfect. . . . One could give or take away valve travel at will perfectly. . . . When an engine will tackle 17 corridor coaches from Salisbury to Exeter as I did once as a young driver on a Saturday prior to August Bank Holiday when traffic was very heavy, it is a good bit of machinery.' *(George Harrison/D.J. Hucknall Collection)*

Opposite, top: With the shed in the background, this view of the yard at Salisbury was taken at 1.15 p.m. on 16 June 1957. In the yard were rebuilt 'Merchant Navy' Class No. 35009 *Shaw Savill*, a Salisbury locomotive at the time, and unrebuilt 'West Country' Class No. 34033 *Chard*. The ten-road shed was opened in 1901 and was built according to LSWR practice at the time with glazed gable ends. By the early 1950s the roof was in a poor state of repair and British Railways patched the front up with corrugated asbestos sheeting, leaving the rear gables glazed. *(David Holmes)*

Opposite, bottom: The yard of the engine shed at Dover Marine is shown on 14 July 1950. The locomotives are P Class 0–6–0T No. 31027 (allocated to Ashford), 'West Country' Class No. 34101 *Hartland* and N15 Class ('King Arthur') No. 30767 *Sir Valence* (both probably allocated to Stewarts Lane). From the headcode of No. 34101, it had been working a Victoria to Folkestone/Dover train. Oliver Bulleid mentioned such workings in a letter to George Harrison. He wrote, 'The Stewarts Lane men had a very heavy job of working the trains down to Dover and back, and made a wonderful job when called upon to do anything out of the way.' The N15 could have worked a heavy Ostend boat express. *(H.C. Casserley)*

Kingmoor 'Black 5' No. 45466 is seen here on
7 August 1961 at the south end of its home shed.
Kingmoor was an eight-road through-shed, and
the road occupied by No. 45466 is 'No. 1',
according to the identification number on the
end wall above and to the left of the locomotive
tender. No. 45466 was allocated to Kingmoor in
August 1952, having been a Perth engine prior
to that. It remained a Kingmoor engine
throughout the 1950s and into the early 1960s.
(D.J. Hucknall Collection)

Standing at the entrance to Perth shed on 6 March 1965 were 'Britannia' Class No. 70038 *Robin Hood* and BR Standard Class No. 73148. The latter engine was based at St Rollox throughout its working life. Initially allocated there in March 1957, it was withdrawn in September 1965. No. 70038 was added to Kingmoor's stock in January 1964. It was withdrawn from service in August 1967. *(D.J. Hucknall)*

Opposite, top: D34 Class No. 62485 *Glen Murran* stood in the yard at the former Caledonian Railway shed at Dundee West on 29 July 1953. According to Hawkins and Reeve (1987), this shed 'shared, with Ferryhill, a curiously inconsequential status'. At the end of 1947 it had fifteen engines in its allocation, but Tay Bridge shed, only a matter of yards away, absorbed its engines and men on Nationalisation. The shed lasted throughout the 1950s as a storage/stabling point for locomotives. No. 62485 (as No. 9241) was built in 1919. Throughout its LNER days it was an Eastfield engine. After Nationalisation it was transferred to Dunfermline. *(David Holmes)*

Opposite, bottom: 'Britannia' Pacific No. 70010 (formerly *Owen Glendower*) was seen in the yard at Perth mpd on the evening of Sunday 27 June 1965. At the time, the locomotive was in one of the sidings to the north end of the shed's offices, close to the repair shops. To the right of the locomotive are refractory bricks and other spares for locomotive servicing. When new in October 1951, No. 70010 was sent to Norwich, from where, together with other 'Britannias', it worked passenger trains between Liverpool Street and Norwich via either Ipswich or Cambridge. C.J. Allen (in *The Railway Magazine*, 1958) described a run with the 'Essex Coast Express' during which No. 70010 (plus eight coaches) ran from Shenfield to Witham in, he surmised, the fastest time (14 minutes and 5 seconds) that had been recorded in his articles. *(D.J. Hucknall)*

A row of former Caledonian Railway tank engines stands at Corkerhill shed on 22 July 1959. Leading the line is McIntosh 782 Class 0–6–0T No. 56364, followed by an unidentifiable McIntosh 478 Class outside-cylinder 0–6–0T. Behind the locomotives are two blocks of houses, probably in Corkerhill Terrace, that were part of the 'model village' of 132 houses built by the Glasgow and South Western Railway for the staff of the depot. It was a laudable example of foresight and responsibility by the railway company. 'The Village' remained until the 1950s, when it was replaced by Local Authority flats. *(W.A.C. Smith)*

Opposite, top: A pair of Kingmoor 'Britannias', Nos 70036 (formerly *Boadicea*) and 70008 (formerly *Black Prince*) stood outside the shed at Perth on 24 April 1965. No. 70008 was moved to Kingmoor in December 1963, having previously been at Norwich (April 1951 to September 1961) and March (September 1961 to December 1963). No. 70036 was assigned to Kingmoor in February 1964, having spent the previous month as an Upperby locomotive. *(D.J. Hucknall)*

Opposite, bottom: Carlisle Upperby's 'Black 5' No. 5414 was seen outside Preston mpd on 26 April 1949 together with 'Patriot' Class No. 45519 *Lady Godiva*. At the time, Preston's allocation of locomotives included five other 'Patriots' (Nos 45508/16/24/37/44). Within a couple of years, the 'Patriots' were dispersed, with the exception of *Lady Godiva*, which remained a Preston engine until June 1954. *(H.C. Casserley)*

This view across an almost deserted shed yard at St Margaret's, looking between two of the shed's three water columns towards the sand-drying kiln, was taken on 13 June 1965. The locomotive in front of B1 Class No. 61076 was another B1 – Dundee's No. 61180. About this time, diesel locomotives were becoming increasingly common and the B1s would be used on any working, including goods and 'trip' workings. *(D.J. Hucknall)*

Opposite, bottom: Responsible for some brilliant runs throughout its working life on the East Coast Main Line, A4 Class No. 60007 *Sir Nigel Gresley* was sent to Scotland in 1963. Initially stored at Dalry Road shed, it emerged from storage on 20 July 1964 and was allocated to Aberdeen. From there, it performed with merit on the Glasgow–Aberdeen route until it was withdrawn from service in February 1966. Seen here on 20 March 1965 in the yard at St Margaret's, No. 60007 awaits a duty that will return it to the North. *(D.J. Hucknall)*

An unidentifiable Stanier 'Jubilee' Class and Pickersgill 4P 4–6–2T No. 15354 were seen at Polmadie on 27 October 1945. Of the latter, twelve such engines (LMS Nos 15350–61) were built and frequently used on the Wemyss Bay services, giving rise to the associated name 'Wemyss Bay tank'. *(H.C. Casserley)*

An unidentified A3 and B1 No. 61404 standing in the shed yard at St Margaret's on 14 February 1965. No. 61404 had always been a Scottish locomotive. Initially allocated to Kittybrewster in May 1950, it, together with the other northern B1s, dealt with passenger, fish and goods trains on the main line and the line between Aberdeen and Elgin. No. 61404 was transferred to Haymarket after six months and remained on the allocation there until March 1959. In August 1962 it became a 64A locomotive and performed its duties until November 1965, when it was withdrawn from service and sold to the Motherwell Machinery and Scrap Company. *(D.J. Hucknall)*

Opposite, top: During 1964, a number of A3s were taken out of service, leaving three survivors (Nos 60041/52/100), all allocated to St Margaret's shed. Seen here at its home shed, an exceedingly dirty No. 60052 *Prince Palatine* stands in the shed yard in February 1965. A notable feature on the right of the picture is the shed's sand-drying kiln. No. 60052 had been transferred to 64A in June 1963 from Gateshead, its nineteenth move since 1924! At St Margaret's it was used on various freight duties to Carlisle (via the Waverley route), Newcastle and Dundee. *(D.J. Hucknall)*

Opposite, bottom: B1 Class No. 61307 stood in the yard of the main shed at Dalry Road depot on 20 March 1965. The photograph was taken looking approximately south-east across the lines towards the West End Engine Works and the tenements on Dundee Street. The shed's ash road was located behind the B1 adjacent to the line of wagons on the shed side. *(D.J. Hucknall)*

Dalry Road shed occupied a triangular site defined by the main line, Dalry Road station and the line to Coltbridge Junction, and Dalry Cemetery (or more precisely Coffin Lane). The shed was made up of various buildings. The main one was a four-road structure opened in 1911, possibly on the site of an older (1860s) shed. There was also a two-road wooden structure (marked on a 1950 Ordnance Survey map as an 'Engine Shed' but referred to by Hawkins and Reeve (1987) as a Repair Shop) outside which engines were regularly serviced. On a surprisingly sunny day (13 February 1965) for that winter, 'Black 5' No. 45477 stood in the yard of its home shed. In the background, the signal gantry at Dalry Junction can be seen, while, behind and to the rear of the locomotive, the shed water tank and the chimney, probably for the sand kiln, are visible. *(D.J. Hucknall)*

A close-up of a very work-stained B1 Class No. 61245 *Murray of Elibank* taken outside the main shed building at Dalry Road on 31 January 1965. Very apparent on the running-plate by the smokebox is the locomotive's steam-driven generator. No. 1245 was completed in October 1947 and named at a ceremony at Cowlairs on 17 December 1947 after one of the Scottish directors of the LNER. By late January 1965, No. 61245 was being found any appropriate work. It was, however, withdrawn from service in July of the same year. *(D.J. Hucknall)*

Chapter Five

The Men

Chas and Ted, the crew of 'West Country' Class No. 34018 *Axminster*, were ready to take the locomotive off Salisbury shed towards the station and its next turn of duty. The driver, wearing a collar and tie, and his mate, appropriately dressed for his work, seemed genuinely pleased to be on duty. *(George Harrison/D.J. Hucknall Collection)*

In comparison to some regions of British Railways, the Western Region seemed determined to remove steam working from its lines as soon as it possibly could. The steam era in Cornwall was close to its end by the autumn of 1962. A few out-of-service tank engines could still be seen at Penzance shed in August 1963, but by the spring of the following year not a trace of the steam locomotive remained. In this photograph, taken at a rainy Truro station on 12 July 1965, the driver of 'Warship' Type 4 No. D864 *Zambesi*, on the 12 noon Truro–Bradford train, is looking closely at the photographer. No doubt enjoying far more comfortable working conditions than would have been possible in the days of steam, he was nevertheless wearing the type of clothing worn by generations of drivers before him. *(D.J. Hucknall)*

Opposite, top: 'Patriot' Class No. 45538 *Giggleswick* was used by Nuneaton shed (2B) for an excursion (1Z63) to Blackpool on 19 August 1961. The fireman Don Rutter can be seen assisting his mate, Driver 'Tug' Wilson, oil round the locomotive on the ash pit at Bloomfield Road Sidings, Blackpool. *(The late Don Rutter Collection/Mrs. R. Rutter)*

Opposite, bottom: A discussion was taking place between the crew of Kingmoor Class 9F No. 92093 and those of other locomotives in a train of five locomotives held in a siding near Plumpton signal-box (about 13 miles south of Carlisle). The date was sometime in the late summer of 1967 and the locomotives were returning to Kingmoor coupled together after working engineering trains. No. 92093 had moved to Kingmoor in January 1967 from Kirkby-in-Ashfield. It was withdrawn some eight months later after a total of just ten years in service. *(George Harrison/D.J. Hucknall Collection)*

Locomotive working arrangements at Salisbury were divided into a highly specialised passenger link, a large spare link for various duties and a goods link. At the lower levels were the shed men whose duties involved locomotive preparation and disposal and the movement of engines in and around the shed. Perce Pittman, seen here on the footplate of 'West Country' Class No. 34037 *Clovelly*, was one of the 'p and d' men. As the days of steam came to a close at Salisbury, Mr Pittman would have coped comfortably with his workload. *(George Harrison/D.J. Hucknall Collection)*

Opposite: Although retired at the time of this photograph, Driver Ernest Pistell, suitably dressed, struck a characteristic pose on the footplate of rebuilt 'Battle of Britain' Class No. 34056 *Croydon*. Ernest Pistell had been a top-link driver at Salisbury, and Hawkins and Reeve in their book on former LSWR sheds remarked, 'Salisbury men considered themselves the elite of the line.' They continued, 'The Top Link (at Salisbury) was envied by many depots, twelve turns with nine attracting mileage allowances. All the jobs were to Exeter or London, Salisbury having the best of the Southern main line work.' *(George Harrison/D.J. Hucknall Collection)*

Driver Stoodley posed for the camera beside a BR Standard Class 5 locomotive at Salisbury shed. His working clothes were typical of the time – a 'grease-top' cap with its 'British Railways' badge, blue cotton trousers held up with braces, and a loosely fitting cotton jacket over his shirt and pullover. *(George Harrison/D.J. Hucknall Collection)*

Driver Knight and Fireman Hooper of Salisbury shed were in charge of the last train on the Amesbury branch on 15 May 1965. *(George Harrison/D.J. Hucknall Collection)*

Perce Pittman, one of Salisbury shed's preparation staff, stood on the buffer beam of 'Black 5' No. 45222 on 18 September 1966. According to the locomotive's destination discs (there is a disc behind Mr Pittman's right shoulder), the engine was working a Southampton–Salisbury (via Redbridge) and return train. No. 45222 had an interesting association with the Southern Region. Although a Huddersfield engine for several years (December 1950 to November 1958), it spent a couple of months on loan to Nine Elms (May to July 1953). During 1966, it again spent time in the south. It failed at Bournemouth on 31 August of that year with the 8.30 a.m. Newcastle–Poole train. Although back on duty when seen here, it spent a considerable amount of time at Eastleigh shed, being used as required. It was eventually returned, light engine, to the LM Region on 24 December 1966. *(George Harrison/D.J. Hucknall Collection)*

A4 Class locomotive No. 60006 *Sir Ralph Wedgwood* was being checked by its driver at Perth depot on 16 August 1964. As No. 4466 *Herring Gull* (renamed in January 1944), the locomotive was allocated to King's Cross Top Shed in August 1944. When King's Cross shed closed in June 1963, No. 60006, together with the shed's other A4s, was transferred to New England depot. Four months later, it was re-allocated to St Margaret's but initially stored at Dalry Road. In May 1964, No. 60006 became an Aberdeen engine, operating on the Glasgow–Aberdeen, former Caledonian Railway, main line. Aberdeen and Perth railwaymen liked the A4s, and No. 60006 handled the work competently. It was out of action at Ferryhill in mid-August 1965 and was withdrawn shortly afterwards. *(D.J. Hucknall)*

Opposite: Driver Marsh and his fireman are seen on the footplate of 'West Country' Class No. 34001 *Exeter* at Salisbury station. The date was 8 January 1966, when the locomotive was heading a privately sponsored Waterloo–Guildford–Fareham–Salisbury special. *(D.J. Hucknall Collection)*

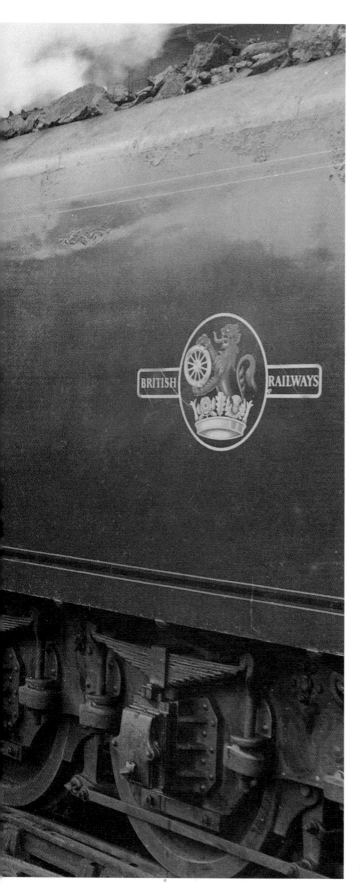

One of the crew of A4 Class No. 60025 *Falcon* contemplated the road as the locomotive left King's Cross station, crossing from Platform 10 towards the Down main line and Gas Works Tunnel. As No. 4484, *Falcon* entered service in February 1937 at Haymarket shed. After two years, the locomotive was re-allocated to King's Cross where, apart from two interludes at Grantham, it spent most of its working life. At King's Cross there were, over a number of years, close associations between certain locomotives and drivers. Just as Driver Ted Hailstone and *Silver Link* were paired, *Falcon*'s regular driver was Percy Howard. *(D.J. Hucknall Collection)*

In his book *North Eastern Locomotive Sheds*, Hoole commented that 'very little has been written about the sheds themselves and the people who, over the years, have toiled and sweated in primitive conditions'. He continued, 'And conditions certainly were bad, often with primitive sanitary facilities and none of the current amenity blocks. One shed I knew had a single water tap and a small corner washbasin for more than 30 men.' This photograph, taken by Hubert Casserley at Saltley on 2 March 1935, could have formed the basis of Hoole's comments years later. *(H.C. Casserley)*

Opposite: Eight days after the photograph of A4 Class No. 60024 *Kingfisher* was taken at Carstairs shed, the locomotive headed an LCGB special, 'The A4 Commemorative Rail Tour'. Here, on 27 March 1966, the valve gear of No. 60024 is closely scrutinised by the Southern Region pilot driver who assisted the North Eastern crew with the locomotive. *Kingfisher* was withdrawn on 5 September 1966, when the use of A4s on the Glasgow–Aberdeen trains came to an end. In his book on the latter days of steam on this line, Welch (1993) referred to the log of a fast Down run made by No. 60024 in July 1966 in which Perth to Forfar (32½ miles) was covered in 29 minutes and the remainder of the journey was similarly speedy. He wrote, 'As the passengers alighted from the train, there must have been a few wistful backward glances, in the realization that this could really be one of the last runs in normal service.' *(George Harrison/ D.J. Hucknall Collection)*

George Harrison had a great admiration for O.V.S. Bulleid and his locomotives. He corresponded regularly with Bulleid during the mid- and late 1960s and worked tirelessly in the collection of testimonials from the drivers on their recollections of working with the original Pacifics. Two bound volumes were compiled and presented to Oliver Bulleid on different occasions. This photograph shows George Harrison presenting a testimonial to Bulleid. In a letter to Mr Harrison on 11 March 1967, Bulleid wrote, 'You are wonderful the way you are getting the testimonials together: it will be a source of pride to all the family as well as Southern enthusiasts when completed.' *(The late R.L. Curl/D.J. Hucknall Collection)*

O.V.S. Bulleid seen at the presentation of drivers' testimonials at Exmouth Junction. He is holding the notes for his speech.

Chapter Six

Portraits

'Battle of Britain' Class No. 34052 *Lord Dowding* had a long association with Salisbury shed, having probably been part of the allocation there from at least 1949 to 1967. Its emergence from rebuilding in September 1958 produced the fine locomotive shown here. Bulleid's opinion of the rebuilding programme has been mentioned elsewhere in this book, but C.J. Allen was also bemused. Writing in *Modern Railways* in September 1962, he remarked, 'it is impossible to avoid the conclusion that little use is being made of the developments in speed and haulage made possible by the Bulleid Pacifics, especially since their rebuilding. Apart from the Down and Up "ACE" . . . there is scarcely a single assignment on the Western District of the Southern Region that imposes any tax at all on the haulage capacity of these outstanding machines.' *(D.J. Hucknall Collection)*

'Battle of Britain' Class No. 34051 *Winston Churchill* entered service in December 1946. It was a Salisbury engine of long standing, having been on its allocation since at least March 1949. Here it is seen at its home shed in April 1965. On 30 January 1965, No. 34051 was used to pull the special train that carried Winston Churchill's coffin, for burial at Bladon, from Waterloo to Hanborough. On the footplate that day were Driver A.W. Hurley and his mate, 22-year-old Fireman J.C. Lester. No. 34051 was withdrawn in September 1965. It was stored at Salisbury for a few months with its name-plates and coupling rods removed before being restored. *(George Harrison/D.J. Hucknall Collection)*

Opposite, top: Unrebuilt 'West Country' Class No. 34006 *Bude* (72A from May 1949, Nine Elms April 1951 to 1964, Salisbury from 1964) is seen in the shed yard at Salisbury. The locomotive entered traffic in August 1945 and was withdrawn in March 1967, a relatively long life for an unrebuilt Bulleid 4–6–2. These locomotives had some excellent points and many shortcomings. At some depots, particularly Exmouth Junction, they were regarded with affection. In a letter to George Harrison in October 1966, a Mr Pridham referred to the 'supreme qualities of Mr Bulleid's Pacifics', although criticism was levelled at the reverser and the driver's lookout window which, in heavy rain or fog, gave dreadful visibility. *(George Harrison/D.J. Hucknall Collection)*

Opposite, bottom: Looking in very good order, unrebuilt 'West Country' Class No. 34019 *Bideford* is seen moving out of the shed yard at Eastleigh. The locomotive had been allocated to Brighton for several years but, as with all that shed's Light Pacifics, No. 34019 was transferred in September 1963, initially to Salisbury. It hauled the 'last' steam train to Exeter (for the Southern Counties Touring Society) on 13 November 1966. From his correspondence in the late 1960s, Oliver Bulleid appeared very irritated by criticism of his designs for the Pacifics and considered many comments to be ill-informed. An example appears in a letter to George Harrison dated 19 November 1966, when Bulleid wrote, 'Mr Smith, in his letter, spoke of chain stretch and this I think must be a confusion with what I believe to be correct, namely, that the links bed down onto the pins and it is this that results in the sag of the chain. It would require very high forces indeed to stretch the links themselves. I feel sure I told you that when the Eastleigh Works Manager reported to me this sagging, the makers asked me to tell him to hang up, side-by-side, from an overhead crane, the chain complained about and a new one and then let me know the difference he found. He did, and found none.' *(D.J. Hucknall Collection)*

'Battle of Britain' Class No. 34089 *602 Squadron* was standing outside Salisbury shed, possibly on 18 June 1967, when it worked the RCTS 'Farewell to Southern Steam' train from Southampton to Weymouth. No. 34089 received the last official classified locomotive repair at Eastleigh Works and returned to service on 6 October 1966 after suitable ceremony. It was, nevertheless, withdrawn on 9 July 1967 and stored at Salisbury until March 1968 – one of the last steam locomotives on the Southern Region. *(George Harrison/D.J.Hucknall Collection)*

Opposite, top: The locomotive shed at Salisbury faced approximately ENE. In the spring and early autumn, the late-afternoon sun illuminated superbly locomotives in the yard. Here, in September 1965, 'Battle of Britain' Class No. 34066 *Spitfire* makes a fine portrait. The route-indication discs above the buffer beam of the locomotive suggested that it was probably involved in a Salisbury–Portsmouth and return working. *(George Harrison/D.J. Hucknall Collection)*

Opposite, bottom: Briefly (February to March 1964), 'Jubilee' Class No. 45697 *Achilles* was a Farnley Junction engine. It is seen here on its home shed on 10 March 1964. No. 45697 was one of the 'Jubilees' involved in the London Midland–Scottish Region transfers in August 1952, moving from Blackpool to Carlisle Kingmoor. Evidence of an overhaul at St Rollox can be seen in the form of the large cab-side numerals. The locomotive returned to Blackpool's allocation in August 1962 and my only sight of it was at the rear of Blackpool shed in April 1963. *(David Holmes)*

'A4' Class No. 60031 *Golden Plover* (LNER No. 4497) was initially allocated to Haymarket in October 1937 and remained an Edinburgh locomotive until February 1962, when it was moved to St Rollox/Balornock to participate in trials of a 3-hour schedule for trains to Aberdeen. No. 60031 suffered a serious failure and No. 60027 *Merlin* was substituted. The trial was satisfactory, and from 18 June 1962 the accelerated Glasgow–Aberdeen service began with St Rollox locomotives working 'The Grampian' to Aberdeen, returning in the afternoon with 'The Granite City'. In this photograph No. 60031, looking to be in fine condition, is seen leaving Waverley station on 18 April 1965 with an SLS special from Glasgow to Carlisle via the Waverley route. *Golden Plover* worked throughout that summer but failed at Perth with 'The Grampian'. It returned to service after repair but was withdrawn in October 1965.

Opposite, top: One of Polmadie's 'Duchesses', No. 46232 *Duchess of Montrose*, is seen in the yard of its home shed on 8 May 1954. Polmadie's Pacifics were rarely seen south of Crewe, but worked expresses between Crewe and Glasgow/Perth. In the late 1940s/early 1950s, such workings would have included the 7.30 p.m. from Euston to Perth, and the Inverness and Glasgow sleepers. *(W.A.C. Smith)*

Opposite, bottom: A2 No. 60529 *Pearl Diver* of Haymarket shed, Edinburgh, would have been a very infrequent visitor to the South. According to records, No. 60529 had a general overhaul at Doncaster in early 1959 (22 January to 6 March). The locomotive, however, appeared to be relatively fresh from the Works when it was photographed at New England on 26 May 1959. *(K.C.H. Fairey)*

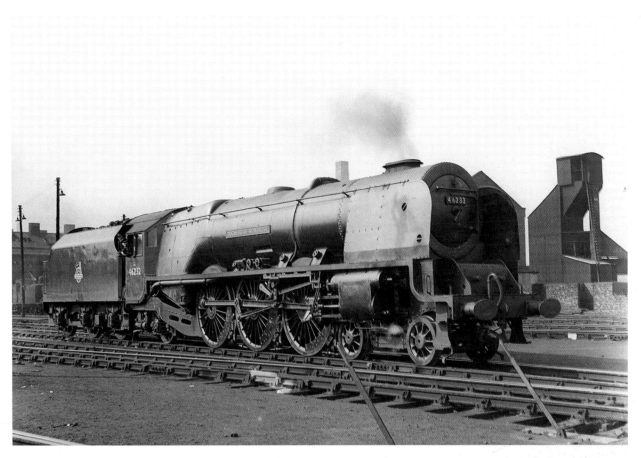

2P Class 4–4–0 No. 40411 (19A, Sheffield Grimesthorpe) is seen at Millhouses shed (19B) in March 1953. Millhouses shed had eight roads and was opened in 1901. It provided passenger locomotives for the Sheffield area. For example, at the end of November 1960 its allocation included two rebuilt 'Patriots' (Nos 45514/36), twelve 'Jubilees' (45570/6/90/94, 45602/7/27/54/56/64/83, 45725) and four 'Royal Scots' (Nos 46131/47/48/51). The shed closed on 1 January 1962 but the building remains. *(J.C. Hillmer)*

The Caley 'Jumbos' were designed by Drummond in 1883 and had the LMS power classification 2F. They were built over a period of fourteen years and No. 57398, seen here in excellent condition at Hamilton shed, was an example of the post-1895 batch. No. 57398 had been a Hamilton engine of long standing, but it was moved on to Motherwell in September 1959. *(W.A.C. Smith)*

Locomotive classes usually associated with Scotland appeared occasionally well south of the border for various long-term duties. McIntosh 'Caley Pug' 0–4–0ST, LMS No. 16027, was one such locomotive. It is seen here at an unidentifiable location, possibly Shrewsbury, after being loaned to that shed in January 1936. It spent a number of years at Trench (a sub-shed of Shrewsbury) before being moved to Preston in October 1950. By May 1954, however, its work there had been taken over by No. 47008. Eventually, in January 1957, it was acquired by Crewe Works for general duties. It was withdrawn in October 1960. *(D.J. Hucknall Collection)*

Class J36 No. 65287, shown here at Thornton Junction shed on 25 April 1965, had been a Kipps engine modified to operate on the Gartverrie Quarry line near Glenboig (once famous for its fireclay refractory bricks). On that line was a low bridge under the main line. So severe was the height restriction that two J36s (Nos 65285 and 87) had their chimneys, domes and cabs reduced in height to accommodate the bridge. No. 65287 was transferred from Kipps to St Rollox in October 1962, possibly because of the closure of the Gartverrie line, and then to Grangemouth in May 1963. It was stored at Grangemouth until April 1964, when it was moved to Thornton Junction. Within two months of this photograph it was withdrawn – the last surviving steam locomotive to have been allocated to Kipps. *(D.J. Hucknall)*

V2 Class No. 60970 stood in the shed yard at St Margaret's on 14 February 1965. At the start of that year the Scottish Region had thirteen V2s – eight at St Margaret's and five at Dundee. *(D.J. Hucknall)*

Opposite, top: Looking relatively fresh from overhaul, Eastfield's K2 Class No. 61788 *Loch Rannoch* was taking water at its home shed on 8 September 1956. As No. 4698, No. 61788 was one of the original batch (Nos 4691–4704) of K2s initially allocated to Eastfield. The engines were principally employed on passenger services between Glasgow and Fort William and Mallaig. They also worked goods and fish trains on the West Highland line. 65A's K2s also worked express goods to Edinburgh. The shed, opened by the North British Railway in 1904, was a large fourteen-road through-shed. It outlasted all other sheds on the north side of Glasgow, closing in 1992. At closure, the depot logo was a West Highland terrier. The staff held a farewell ceremony under the title 'The Dug is Deid'. *(W.A.C. Smith)*

Opposite, bottom: An excellent portrait of V4 Class 2–6–2 No. 61700 *Bantam Cock* on 9 May 1953 at Eastfield depot, where the locomotive was then allocated. When initially introduced in 1941, the locomotive was sent to Doncaster. It was then transferred to York (19 April 1941), Haymarket (3 May 1941), Stratford (21 June 1941) and Norwich (August 1941). The engine went to the Scottish Area in February 1942. *Bantam Cock* was transferred to Eastfield from Haymarket in October 1943, initially working on the West Highland line and, latterly, on general goods work. On 24 May 1954, No. 61700 (and its sister No. 61701) moved to Ferryhill shed, Aberdeen. No. 61700 was withdrawn in May 1957. *(W.A.C. Smith)*

A4 Class No. 60010 *Dominion of Canada* (formerly No. 4489 *Woodcock*; allocations: King's Cross, May 1937; Grantham, April 1957; New England, June 1963; Aberdeen, October 1963) had apparently failed when seen at Perth shed on 5 March 1965. The locomotive is seen here in one of the short sidings at the rear of the depot. With extraordinary kindness, one of the shed staff had reversed the engine out of the shed so that I could photograph it. Early in May that year, it was sent to Darlington for an Intermediate Heavy Repair but, due to the poor condition of the boiler, it was condemned. Rather than being cut up, it languished at Bank Top shed until August 1966, when it was moved to Crewe Works and cosmetically restored. On 10 April 1967 it was formally presented to the Acting High Commissioner for Canada and now resides in the Canadian Railroad Historical Museum near Montreal. *(D.J. Hucknall)*

Opposite, top: Peppercorn A1 Class No. 60157 *Great Eastern* was seen at the Old Engine Shed at Grantham on 4 October 1953. The structure to the left of the A1 is the old coaling stage. No. 60157 was allocated to Grantham for five years (September 1951 to September 1956). It was one of five of the class (Nos 60153–7) to be fitted with roller bearings and, as such, to be referred to in the Presidential Address to the Institute of Locomotive Engineers in 1961 as, 'the kind of locomotive Sir Nigel Gresley would have designed had he still been alive'. *(J. C. Hillmer)*

Opposite, bottom: A3 Class No. 60108 *Gay Crusader* was a King's Cross engine when seen at the south end of New England shed on 7 July 1960, and this is reflected in its external condition. It was ready to work a return 'named' express (note the reversed headboard on the top boiler bracket). The A3s were fine-looking locomotives, as can be seen, and Coster, in J.F. Clay's anthology (*Essays in Steam*, 1970), remarked, 'the "A3s" are amongst the most handsome locomotives ever to be built. There has rarely been such a perfect blend of grace and power.' No. 60108 had been fitted with a double chimney in May 1959. Approximately one month after this photograph was taken, it was called for a general overhaul at Doncaster. *(K.C.H. Fairey)*

A fine photograph of 'Jubilee' Class No. 45673 *Keppel* taken at St Rollox shed in March 1953. No. 45673 was transferred from Preston to Kingmoor in October 1952. It became a Perth locomotive in February of the following year, remaining on the allocation until June 1960, when it moved to Corkerhill. This photograph, taken looking approximately west, shows an intermediate stage in the replacement of the smoke vents on the shed roof. To the right of the 'Black 5' the rather striking originals can be seen, while above the tender and cab of No. 45673 the probably more efficient corrugated asbestos replacement is clearly seen. *(John Robertson/The Transport Treasury)*

Opposite, top: In what was reportedly the usual state of cleanliness for New England shed's locomotives in the latter days of steam, A3 No. 60108 *Gay Crusader* waited for her next duty outside her home shed on 16 May 1963. The locomotive was on that shed's allocation from 10 September 1961 to 16 June 1963. It had emerged from a casual light overhaul at Doncaster some three months earlier, but by October 1963 the locomotive had been withdrawn. *(K.C.H. Fairey)*

Opposite, bottom: A3 Class No. 60112 *St Simon*, a Grantham engine at the time, was photographed at its home shed on 18 April 1963. It was standing outside the 'Top' (or 'new') shed. No. 60112 remained on the allocation until 8 September 1963, when it was transferred to Doncaster and, finally, to New England. I last saw No. 60112 at Waverley station, Edinburgh, on Christmas Eve 1964. It was condemned two days later. *(K.C.H. Fairey)*

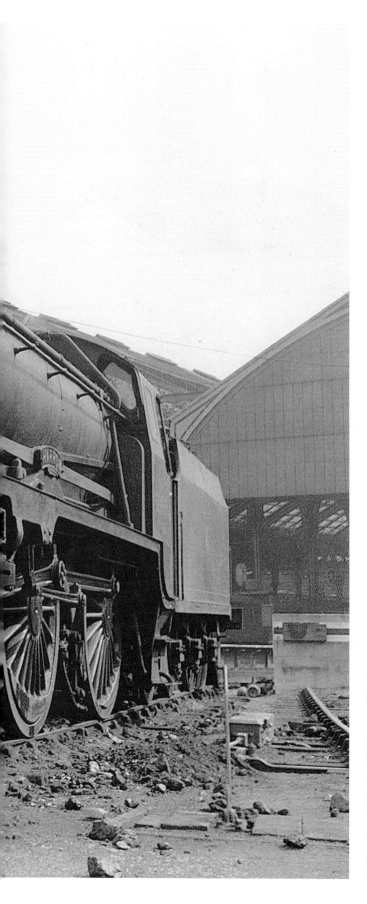

Maunsell V ('Schools') Class locomotive No. 30919 *Harrow* is seen in the shed yard at Brighton, with the station in the background. The design for the 'Schools' Class came in response to a request from the Running Department of the Southern Railway for engines that were capable of hauling 400-ton trains at an average speed of 55mph within the limits imposed by the line to Hastings. The result was an outstanding locomotive, which probably ranked as one of the finest 4–4–0s ever to run in Britain. Although the class was mainly employed on the line from Victoria to the Kent coast and the route to Hastings, some, such as No. 30919, were allocated to Brighton and worked over the Central Section of the Southern Region. *(H.G. Usmar/ D.J. Hucknall Collection)*

A striking shot of a BR Standard Class 4 4–6–0, fitted with a double chimney, as it stood in the shed yard at Salisbury. The Class 4s were built at Swindon and had a relatively short life (1951–68). The first Class 4 to receive a double chimney was No. 75029 in June 1957. The power of the locomotive was improved significantly and engines thus modified were often used on duties where weight restrictions precluded Class 5s but demanded the equivalent power. Unusually, this locomotive retained fluted coupling rods, although these over time tended to be replaced by those having a rectangular cross-section. *(George Harrison/ D.J. Hucknall Collection)*

St Rollox Works' shunter, 0F 0–4–0ST No. 56025, was dwarfed by Corkerhill's 'Black 5' No. 45251 as it went about its duties at St Rollox on 5 July 1957. No. 56025 was, as can be seen, immaculately maintained. It was withdrawn in May 1960. *(H.C. Casserley)*

Chapter Seven

Duties

61XX Class 2–6–2T No. 6113 was standing at Platform 6 of Paddington station when seen in 1960. At the time the engine was allocated to Old Oak Common shed, although it was transferred to Didcot later in the year. The 61XX Class were regular performers on local passenger turns in an area covering London, Berkshire and Oxfordshire, working from sheds such as Slough, Southall, Reading and Oxford. *(H.G. Usmar/D.J. Hucknall Collection)*

Doncaster's A2/3 Class No. 60523 *Sun Castle* prepares to leave King's Cross station. No. 60523 was a Doncaster engine from January 1960 until September 1962, when it was transferred, for the third time in its working life, to New England depot. When new (August 1947), *Sun Castle* was allocated to King's Cross Top Shed and would have been used on a variety of main-line duties. In May 1948 it was moved to Copley Hill and then, within the same month (December 1948), to Grantham via New England. It returned to New England in April 1959. The movement of locomotives from shed to shed may have seemed random, and it gave rise to a brief but fascinating correspondence in the *Journal of the Engine Shed Society*. It was concluded that there was always a valid reason and that did not include 'getting rid of rubbish'. In the case of No. 60523, it may have been due to reallocation of work and the introduction of the Peppercorn A1s. A correspondent in the *Journal* remarked, 'Just look at the number of times the workings were altered over the years on the East Coast main line with engine changing at Grantham and Peterborough being abandoned, then re-instated, and then only partially done.' *(H.G. Usmar/D.J. Hucknall Collection)*

'Britannia' Class No. 70038 *Robin Hood* is featured elsewhere in this book. When new in 1953, it was allocated to Stratford shed. Subsequent moves took it to Norwich, March and Immingham. Eventually, in December 1963, it was moved to Carlisle, initially to Upperby shed and, in February 1964, to Kingmoor. Seen here probably in 1965, No. 70038 makes a brisk departure from Carlisle to the south. *(George Harrison/D.J. Hucknall Collection)*

Class 8F (as Standard 9Fs converted at the conclusion of the Crosti experiment were classified) No. 92022, probably allocated to Wellingborough at the time, was dashing along the Down main line north of Rotherham Masborough station at 8.30 p.m. on 23 July 1963. No. 92022 was one of ten 9Fs (92020–9) to be built with Franco-Crosti boilers. As an experiment in coal-saving the trial was a failure, and conversion to conventional operation began in September 1959. It was withdrawn from Birkenhead shed in November 1967. *(D.J. Hucknall)*

The Bulford branch was a single line between Grateley and Amesbury. It was opened to military traffic on 1 October 1901 and for a general goods service on 26 April 1902. The last train on the Amesbury branch pulled out on 15 May 1965 headed by a surprisingly dirty 'Battle of Britain' Class No. 34057 *Biggin Hill* of Salisbury shed. *(George Harrison/D.J. Hucknall Collection)*

Dalry Road 'Black 5' No. 44702 (formerly of St Rollox and Eastfield sheds) had been performing morning shunting duties in the private sidings off the former Caledonian Railway's branch between Leith East and Seafield Junction when photographed on 21 January 1965. It was facing in the direction of Seafield and later dashed away with a few trucks and vans. *(D.J. Hucknall)*

This photograph of 'Jubilee' No. 45581 *Bihar and Orissa* was taken at Mirfield, probably in the spring of 1953. It may have been heading a Liverpool–Newcastle train. No. 45581 was one of the locomotives involved in the north–south reshuffle of 'Jubilees' in 1952 which delighted contemporary enthusiasts. The engine was reportedly moved from Kingmoor to Farnley Junction in September 1952, although it seems to have been having a heavy general overhaul at St Rollox Works from 15 August until 31 December 1952. *(E. Blakey/D.J. Hucknall Collection)*

Kingmoor 'Britannia' No. 70035 *Rudyard Kipling* slipped as it was leaving Carlisle station for the south in late 1964. As a new engine in December 1952, it was allocated to Norwich. It became a Kingmoor engine in June 1963 and was withdrawn from service in December 1967. Writing in *Trains Illustrated* in September 1960, C.J. Allen said of the 'Britannias', 'The steam raising capacity of the "Britannia" boiler is now common knowledge; given hard work in firing there seems to be scarcely any limit to what these boilers will produce.' *(George Harrison/D.J. Hucknall Collection)*

Thompson Class A2/3 No. 60513 *Dante* waited to leave King's Cross station at the head of a Down train. Thompson's Pacifics had driving wheels of 6ft 2in diameter and cylinders that were set back between the bogie and leading coupled wheels, giving them a slightly odd look. In spite of current thought on these locomotives, *The Railway Magazine* in May/June 1945 published a note referring to 'the enthusiastic appreciation by the crews of the new Thompson class "A2" Pacifics of the LNER and particularly of such equipment as the rocking grates, hopper ashpans and power reversing gear'. Initially allocated to King's Cross, No. 60513 was sent to New England shed together with other A2/3s as the Peppercorn A1s came into service and assumed many top-link duties. In any event, as reported in *The Railway Magazine*, the A2/3s were 'designed for mixed traffic and heavy grade service, rather than for high-speed passenger work'. *(H.G. Usmar/D.J. Hucknall Collection)*

Opposite, top: A gleaming 'A3' No. 60110 *Robert the Devil* is seen at King's Cross station. Justifiably proud, its driver poses by the locomotive. No. 60110 was allocated to just three sheds (Grantham, King's Cross and, briefly (January to October 1942), New England). With modified blast pipes and Kylchap exhausts, the A3s performed some fine work during the period 1957–61 on trains to Newcastle and Leeds. The RCTS publication on the A3s (*Locomotives of the LNER, Part 2A, Tender Engines – Classes A1–A10*) remarked that, during this period, 'As the weeks went by, the continued excellence of the A3's work was a joy to behold.' Inevitably, with increasing dieselisation, the A3s became redundant. No. 60110 was withdrawn from service in May 1963. *(H.G. Usmar/D.J. Hucknall Collection)*

Opposite, bottom: The rarely photographed 'Britannia' No. 70001 *Lord Hurcombe* was transferred to Carlisle Kingmoor from Aston in October 1964. For approximately ten years, it was one of the locomotives that transformed services on the Great Eastern section of British Railways. From new it was allocated to Stratford, but it was transferred to Norwich in January 1959. It is as a Norwich engine that it is seen here at Liverpool Street station. Of the 'Britannias', Richard Hardy (in Derry's *Book of BR Standards*, Irwell Press 1997) said: 'They were liked by everybody for they were powerful, fast, economical.' Of No. 70001, he went on to say, 'One evening, late in 1955, Dick Brock and Billy Hart lost 45 minutes getting to Shenfield . . . but these were isolated incidences in years of first-class work.' *(H.G. Usmar/D.J. Hucknall Collection)*

The clock on the tower of Southampton Civic Centre was showing 3.15 p.m. when this photograph of 'Merchant Navy' Class No. 35003 (formerly *Royal Mail*) was taken as the locomotive paused at the station in the summer of 1967. The working was probably the Bournemouth–Waterloo duty No. 385, part of which involved the 2.30 p.m. departure from Bournemouth Central. The locomotive was worked by a Nine Elms crew to Waterloo, where Bournemouth men took over. They worked the engine back to Bournemouth and then stabled the locomotive on the shed there. *(George Harrison/D.J. Hucknall Collection)*

Chapter Eight

The End

In the last three months of steam workings on the Southern Region, Salisbury mpd was involved with very few. Having been almost empty, however, the use of the shed as a collection point for steam locomotives on their way to scrapyards in South Wales led to a large increase in locomotive numbers. They began arriving in the last week of steam operation from Nine Elms, Eastleigh, Guildford and Basingstoke. An eye-witness report (Bird 1987) described the scene: 'Lots and lots of steam engines were coming to Salisbury and the shed was full to the brim by the Sunday night. They were mainly dirty, with little paint on them, "West Countries" and "Channel Packets" with nameplates missing and most of the others with no number plates.' Here, 'West Country' Class No. 34025 (formerly *Whimple*) and 'USA' Class No. 30071 are part of an array of locomotives waiting to be moved. They were usually sent in batches, a few at a time, to Newport and elsewhere. *(George Harrison/ D.J. Hucknall Collection)*

Carlisle Kingmoor shed was closed on 1 January 1968. It remained intact for a few months, as this photograph taken in September 1968 shows. *(George Harrison/D.J. Hucknall Collection)*

Opposite, top: Rebuilt 'West Country' Class No. 34018 (formerly *Axminster*) was one of the last locomotives to leave Salisbury to be scrapped. Here it is seen outside the shed on the night of 15 March 1968. On the ground beside the driving wheels are the coupling and connecting rods, which had been removed earlier in the day. Behind the tender is a mineral wagon to receive the coal which was to be removed from it. *(George Harrison/D.J. Hucknall Collection)*

Opposite, bottom: A further example of the late George Harrison's excellent night photography shows 'Battle of Britain' Class No. 34087 *245 Squadron* with its removed coupling and connecting rods lying beside it at Salisbury depot. The locomotive is very dirty, with the cab number barely readable. No. 34087 had been withdrawn from Eastleigh shed, and Salisbury was merely a staging-post on its journey to South Wales for scrapping. *(George Harrison/D.J. Hucknall Collection)*

Two 'Manor' Class locomotives, including No. 7821 *Ditcheat Manor*, were awaiting disposal at Woodham's Scrapyard in South Wales in September 1968. Having had the visit described by George Harrison, Oliver Bulleid replied, 'The Scrap Yard must have been a saddening sight. Have you ever heard why the locomotives were not broken up by the Railways themselves? It seemed a wasteful plan to me as we always recovered so much usable material, especially copper and brass.' *(George Harrison/D.J. Hucknall Collection)*

Opposite: There were to be no further engine arrangements at Salisbury depot. The board, which had once been fixed to the rear wall, had been removed and propped up in the cleared shed. By 1968, Salisbury was used to store withdrawn steam locomotives on their way to scrapyards in South Wales. The depot was demolished in 1969. *(George Harrison/ D.J. Hucknall Collection)*

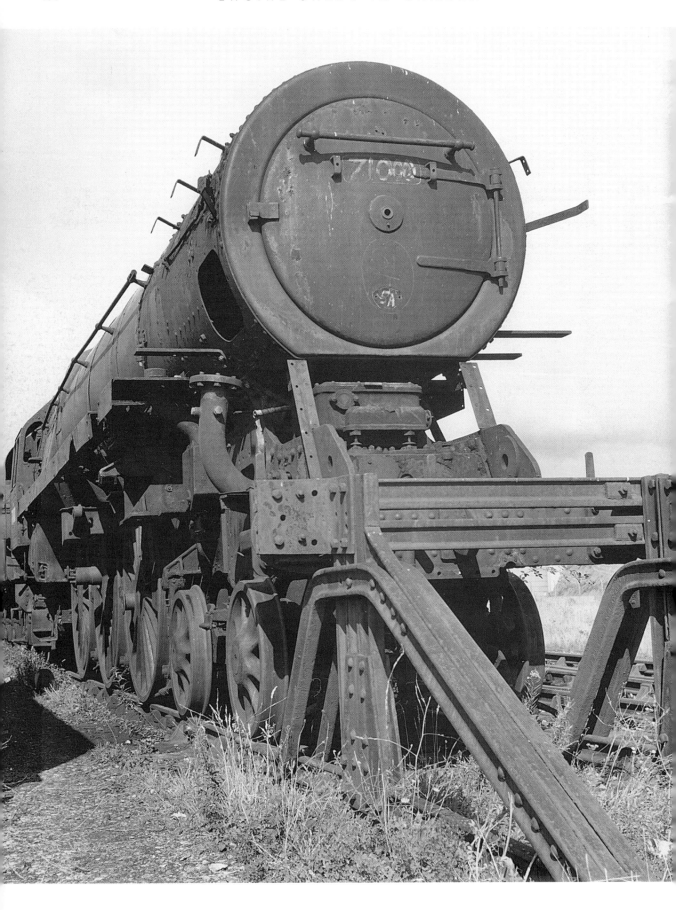

Demolition of the engine shed at Salisbury was in progress in 1969 when this photograph was taken. A report in the *Journal of the Engine Shed Society* in 2000 gave a contemporary account of the site: 'I previously visited the site in 1986 when access was easy. On this occasion (15 August 2000), however, I was unable to get onto the site as the bushes and foliage had become so dense.' The writer continued, however, 'The side and rear walls up to a height of about 5ft still remain on top of the concrete walls in Lower Road and Cherry Orchard Lane.' *(George Harrison/D.J. Hucknall Collection)*

Opposite: British Railways' Class 8P Pacific No. 71000 *Duke of Gloucester* was the last British express passenger steam locomotive to be designed. It was completed in May 1954 and had British Caprotti valve gear. It was allocated to Crewe North depot for most of its working life, apart for a few months at Swindon undergoing tests. These included running trials between Swindon and Westbury via Reading West. Although No. 71000 performed adequately, the boiler showed inexplicable steam deficiencies. Experts were unable to diagnose the problem and it was only years later, during reconstruction, that the origin was identified and the problem rectified. Here, No. 71000 is seen at Woodham's Scrapyard in Barry in September 1968, stripped of cylinders, valve gear, and connecting and coupling rods. *(George Harrison/D.J. Hucknall Collection)*

The name-plate and city coat of arms on unrebuilt 'West Country' Class No. 34002, photographed appropriately on Salisbury shed. George Harrison obtained the name-plate and crest from British Railways and restored them for the City Museum. They were displayed at the opening of the British Railways Staff Association Club, which stood adjacent to the east end of Salisbury station. *(George Harrison/D.J. Hucknall Collection)*

Appendix

One of several 'Merchant Navy' Class locomotives that have survived to the present day is No. 35028 *Clan Line*. Seen here, this fine locomotive was leaving Salisbury on 27 April 1974 with a 'Merchant Navy Preservation Society Special'. In a note to George Harrison in July 1966, Oliver Bulleid wrote, 'In designing the Merchant Navy engines, I did everything I could to make the engines comfortable and easy to handle.' *(G.F. Gilham/D.J. Hucknall Collection)*

This wilderness, seen from the footbridge at the north end of the station in March 1997, was the site of the former Tondu engine shed. The depot was situated in a triangle, one of the apices of which was Tondu station. The shed itself had a manually operated 55ft diameter turntable from which radiated twenty-four roads. One of the shed walls was close to the semaphore signal and ran, approximately, in the direction of the line behind the signal. In its heyday, almost fifty engines were allocated to the shed and 264 men were employed. One wonders how many families were dependent on the wages and salaries generated. *(D.J. Hucknall)*

A view of the former Aberystwyth shed, taken in July 1994, looking to the west, from the site of the turntable. To the right are the remains of the coaling stage with the water tank on the roof. The buildings to the left of the 'Beware of Trains' sign had been the depot offices. British Railways' Aberystwyth shed had been a sub-shed of Machynlleth. It closed in April 1965. It was later converted to accommodate the narrow-gauge engines from the Vale of Rheidol Railway. At the time of the photograph, the shed contained the latter's 2–6–2T No. 7 *Owain Glyndwr. (D.J. Hucknall)*

A reminder of the handsome engine shown at St Rollox elsewhere in this book, this name-plate from 'Jubilee' Class No. 45673 *Keppel* is currently privately owned. *(D.J. Hucknall)*

A remarkable transformation from the rusting hulk photographed in Woodham's Scrapyard. A magnificent No. 71000 *Duke of Gloucester* stands in the yard at Didcot shed on 25 August 1991. It displays the headboard of 'The Mid-day Scot', a train that No. 71000 hauled frequently between Crewe and Glasgow. During the reconstruction of No. 71000, a number of problems that had dogged the locomotive through its British Railways' career were corrected. It was found that the chimney had been wrongly designed and throttled the exhaust steam flow significantly. Further, the damper air-spaces to the ash box were some 470 sq. cm too small. *(D.J. Hucknall)*

Bibliography

Becket, W.S., *The Xpress Locomotive Register, vol. 3, Eastern, North Eastern and Scottish (ex LNER) Regions, 1950–1960*, Xpress Publishing, Caernarvon, June 1999.

Bird, J.H., *Southern Steam Surrender*, Kingfisher Railway Productions, Southampton, 1987.

Bradshaw, T.S., *British Railways Operating History, Southern Region, Part 1, Farnborough to Salisbury*, Xpress Publishing, Caernarvon, 1999.

——, *British Railways Operating History, Southern Region, Part 2, Salisbury to Exeter and the West of England*, Xpress Publishing, Caernarvon, August 1988.

Clay, J.F., *Essays in Steam*, Ian Allan, Shepperton, 1970.

Derry, R., *The Book of the Standards*, Irwell Press, Pinner, 1997.

Griffiths, R., *GWR Sheds in Camera*, Oxford Publishing Co., 1987.

——, *Southern Sheds in Camera*, OPC/ Haynes Publishing Group, 1989.

Griffiths, R. and Hooper, J., *Great Northern Engine Sheds, vol. 1, Southern Area*, Irwell Press, Pinner, 1989.

Hawkins, C. and Reeve, G., *British Railways Engine Sheds, No. 2, A Southern Style*, Irwell Press, Pinner, 1989.

——, *LMS Engine Sheds (Their History and Development), vol. 1, The London North Western Railway*, Wild Swan Publications, Didcot, 1981.

——, *LMS Engine Sheds (Their History and Development), vol. 2, The Midland Railway*, Wild Swan Publications, Upper Bucklebury, 1981.

——, *LMS Engine Sheds (Their History and Development), vol. 5, The Caledonian Railway*, Wild Swan Publications, 1987.

——, *LSWR Engine Sheds, Western District*, Irwell Press, Pinner, 1990.

Hawkins, C., Hooper, J. and Reeve, G., *British Railways Engine Sheds – London Midland Matters*, Irwell Press, Pinner, 1989.

Hoole, K., *North Eastern Railway Sheds*, David & Charles, Dawlish, 1972.

Hooper, J., *LNER Sheds in Camera*, Oxford Publishing Co., 1984.

RCTS (Railway Correspondence and Travel Society), *Locomotives of the LNER, Part 2A, Tender Engines A1–A10*, 4th edn, RCTS, Long Stratton, 1997.

——, *Locomotives of the LNER, Part 2B, Tender Engines Classes B1–B19*, RCTS, Lincoln, 1975.

Taylor, S., *Scenes from the Past 26: Part Four, Return from Blackpool (Central) via the Coast Line*, Foxline Publishing, n.d.

Sixsmith, I., *British Railways Illustrated*, 7, 47 (1997).

Index

Aberystwyth, site 140
accommodation (lodging houses)
    Farnley Junction 9
Alloa 61
Amesbury 124
Ayr 30

Balornock (*see also* St Rollox) 56, 63
Bath (S&DJR) 21
Blackpool 89, 105
Boat of Garten 38
Brighton 118
Bristol
    Barrow Road 37, 60; Bath Road 7, 71
Bulford branch 124
Bulleid, O.V.B. 34,35, 40, 50, 75, 100, 102. 135, 139

Caledonian Railway sheds
    Balornock 22, 56, 79, 106, 117, 120; Carstairs 8; Dalry Road
    36, 85; Dundee West 78; Grangemouth 26; Hamilton 69;
    Kingmoor (Carlisle) 58, 76, 77, 80, 89, 105, 123, 132;
    Motherwell 28; Polmadie 56
Carlisle (Kingmoor) 58, 76, 80, 89, 105, 123, 132
Carstairs 8
coaling facilities
    Alloa 61; Balornock 63; Bath 21; Bristol (Barrow Road) 60;
    (Bath Road) 53, 71; Dundee (Tay Bridge) 67; Farnley
    Junction 63; Grantham 115; Heaton 64; Polmadie 65, 69;
    Preston 62; St Margarets 59; St Rollox 63; Salisbury 66, 68
Corkerhill 68, 81, 117
    shed 81
    terrace 81
Cricklewood 42

Dalry Road shed 36, 69, 85, 86
Dawsholm 23, 24
disposal/preparation 50, 51, 52, 54, 55, 56, 57, 89
Doncaster (Carr Loco) 13, 122
Dover Marine 74
Drivers/firemen
    'Chas and Ted' 87; Dawe 35; Hailstone, E. 97; Hayman, R.
    34, Howard, P. 97; Jeffery 75; Knight and Hooper 92; Marsh
    94; Pistell, E. 90; Pittman, Perce 91, 93; Stoodley 92; on
    'Warship' Class D864 88; Wilson and Rutter 89; Young, J. 69
Dundee (Tay Bridge) 24, 47
Dundee West, 78
duties
    'A2/3' Class No. 60513 128; No. 60523 122; 'A4' Class

No. 60027 59; 'Britannia' Class No. 70035, 127; 70038, 123;
'61XX' Class, 121; '9F' Class No. 92022, 124; 'Warship' Class
diesel 88; Kingmoor 'compounds' 69; Polmadie
'compounds' 69; for Riccarton Junction locomotives 29;
for Salisbury's Class 'N15 66; 'V4' Class 112

Eastfield 37, 112
Eastleigh 11, 41, 73, 93, 102
Exmouth Junction 10

Farnley Junction 9, 55, 63, 105
Fort William 25
'Fouldubs' 26
Fratton 12

Gateshead 16, 84
Glasgow and South Western Railway sheds
    Ayr 30; Corkerhill 81; Greenock (Princes Pier) 23
Grangemouth 26, 72, 111
Grantham
    'new' shed 70, 116; 'old' shed 115; turning triangle 72
Greenock (Princes Pier) 23

Hamilton 69, 110
Harrison, George 34, 40, 50, 75, 100, 102, 138
Hawick 27, 29
Haymarket 71, 97, 106, 107
Heaton 44, 64
Highland Railway
    'Small Ben' 38; 15010 27
Hoole, K. 16, 98
Hull
    Botanic Gardens 42; Dairycoats 39; Springhead 39

Inverness 27

Kingmoor (*see* Carlisle)
Kipps 24, 111

locomotive allocation 122, 125, 127, 128, 129
locomotives
    BR Standards: 'Britannia': 70001, 129; 70008, 80; 70010, 78;
    70035, 127; 70036, 80; 70038, 79, 123; Class '2', 2–6–0: 78050, 28;
    Class '4', 2–6–0: 76013; 76031; 76067, 41; 76069, 73 76100, 26;
    Class '4', 4–6–0: 75059, 11; unidentified, 120; Class '5', 4–6–0:
    73148, 79; Class '4', 2–6–4T 80058, 56; 80133, 73; 80139, 73;
    Class '8P', 4–6–2: 71000, 136, 141; Class '9F', '8F', 2–10–0:
    92022, 124; 92093, 89; 92240, 48

Eastern Region: Class 'A1', 4–6–2: 60145, 16; 60157, 115; Class 'A2', 4–6–2: 60513, 128; 60523, 122; 60529, 107; 60530, 67; Class 'A3', 4–6–2: 60044, 13; 60052, 85; 60057, 71 60073, 64; 60100, 45, 70; 60108, 14, 115, 116; 60110, 129; 60112, 72; Class 'A4', 4–6–2: 60006, 95; 60007, 83; 60010, 114; 60017, 55; 60024, 8, 99; 60025, 96; 60026, 59; 60027, 59; 60031, 106; Class 'B1', 4–6–0: 61076, 82; 61135, 14; 61180, 82; 61199, 44; 61221, 47; 61245,86; 61278, 66; 61307, 85; 61330, 29; 61404, 84; Class 'C16', 4–4–2T: 67489, 27; Class 'D34', 4–4–0: 62485, 78; Class 'G5', 0–4–4T: 67252, 17; Class 'J27', 0–6–0: 65789, 44; 65819, 44; 65858, 44; Class 'J35', 0–6–0: 64494, 27; 64509, 29; Class 'J36', 0–6–0: 65261,29; 65287,111; 65300, 25; 65313, 25; Class 'J37', 0–6–0: 64610, 26; 64617, 61; Class 'J72', 0–6–0T: 69001, 39; Class 'J83', 0–6–0T: 68459, 29; Class 'K2', 2–6–0: 61788, 112; Class 'O2', 2–8–0: 63974, 14; 63984, 72; Class 'V2', 2–6–0: 60801, 18; 60803, 55; 60816, 16 ; 60931, 4, 54; 60970,113; 60979, 18; Class 'V4', 2–6–2: 61700, 112; Class 'Y9', 0–4–0ST: 68114, 24; 9010, 25; 9042, 25; 10095, 25

London Midland Region: 'Black Five', 4–6–0: 5038, 60; 5414, 80; 44702, 125; 44923, 22; 44975, 36; 45122, 63; 45156, 55; 45222, 93; 45251, 120; 45263, 21; 45443, 72; 45466, 76,77; 45477, 37, 86; 'Crab' Class, 2–6–0: 42910, 30; 'Compound', 2P 4–4–0: 40411, 108; 40700, 20; 4P 4–4–0: 1007, 42; 1141, 69; Caledonian 'Pug' 0F, 0–4–0ST: 16027, 110; 56025, 120; Caledonian Class 2F, 0–6–0T: 56129, 56; 'Coronation' Class, 8P 4–6–2: 6224, 65; 46232, 107; Drummond 2F 0–6–0: 57398, 110; Fairburn 2–6–4T: 42691, 23; Ivatt, 4MT 2–6–0: 43048, 9; 'Jubilee' Class, 6P 4–6–0: 5730, 65; 45581, 63, 125; 45673, 117; 45697, 105; McIntosh '139' Class, 3P 4–4–0: 54453, 23; McIntosh '782' Class, 0–6–0T: 56250, 23; 56344, 23; 56364, 81; 'Patriot' Class, 4–6–0: 45508, 62; 45519, 80; 45538, 89; Pickersgill '113' Class, 4–4–0: 54495, 56; Pickersgill, 4P 4–6–2T: 15354, 83; 'Royal Scot' Class, 4–6–0: 46118, 58; '3F' Class, 0–6–0: 3181, 37

Southern Region: 'BB' Class, 4–6–2: 34051, 103; 34052, 51, 101; 34056, 31,90; 34057, 50, 68, 92, 124; 34066, 105; 34087, 133; 34089, 61, 104; 'B4' Class, 0–4–0T: 11; 'H15' Class, 4–6–0: 30488, 12; 'MN' Class, 4–6–2: 35003, 130; 35009, 74; 35010, 10; 35028, 139; 'N' Class, 2–6–0 : 31830, 21; 31867, 21; 'N15, King Arthur' Class, 4–6–0: 30770, 66; 30767, 74; 777, 142 * if used on 'spare' page; 'P' Class, 0–6–0T: 31027, 75; 'U' Class, 2–6–0: 31807, 12; 'USA' Class, 0–6–0T: 30071, 131; 'V, Schools' Class, 4–4–0: 30903, 21; 30919, 118; 'WC' Class, 4–6–2: 34001, 94; 34002, 138; 34005,34; 34006, 35, 102; 34013, 32; 34018, 87, 113; 34019, 102; 34023, 73; 34025, 131; 34026, 44; 34033, 74; 34037, 75,91; 34095, 40; 34097, 11; 34100, 33, 43, 49; 34101, 74; 34104, 40

Western Region: 'Castle' Class, 4–6–0:5029, 142* (if used on p.142) 5069, 52; 5084, 7; 7029, 16; 'Manor' Class, 4–6–0: 7821, 135; 'Modified Hall' Class, 4–6–0: 7903, 71; '43XX' Class, 2–6–0: 4326, 19; '57XX' Class, 0–6–0T: 3607, 19; 8767, 48; 8770, 48; '61XX' Class, 2–6–2T: 6113, 21

Miscellaneous: 'Warship' Class Diesels: D604, 20; D864, 88; D870, 43,46; unidentified, 47

Millhouses 108
Motherwell 28

nameplates: 34002, 138; 45673, 141; 61245, 86
New England 55, 59, 107, 116
North British Railway sheds
 Alloa 61; Dundee (Tay Bridge), 24, 47; Eastfield 37, 112; Fort William 25; Hawick 27; Kipps 24; St Margarets 4, 45; Thornton Junction 29
North Eastern Railway sheds
 Gateshead 16; Hull, Botanic Gardens 42; Hull, Springhead 39; Sunderland, South Dock 17; Tweedmouth 18

Oban 22
Old Oak Common 48

Penzance 20
Perth 27, 69, 78, 79, 80, 95, 114, 117
Polmadie 56, 65, 69, 83, 107
preparation/disposal 4, 56–67, 72, 91, 95
Preston 62, 80
Princes Pier, Greenock 23

Reading South 21
Riccarton Junction 27, 29
Rothesay Dock 23

St Margarets 4, 25, 45, 54, 57, 59, 70, 82, 83, 84, 113
St Rollox/Balornock 22, 56, 79, 106, 117, 120
Salisbury shed 9, 31–5, 40, 41, 43, 44, 46, 47, 49-51, 66, 68, 74, 75, 87, 91, 101, 102, 104, 105, 131
 demolition 134, 137; duties 91; yard 74, 75
Saltley 98
sand-drying kiln 85, 86
Shear legs 72
shed allocation (*see* locomotive allocation)
Southampton Docks shed 11
Stewarts Lane 74
Sunderland, South Dock shed 17

Thornton Junction 29, 111
Tondu, shed site 140
turntables
 Fratton 12; Hawick 27; Haymarket 71; Old Oak Common 48; St Margarets 70
Tweedmouth shed 18

water, facilities 51, 54, 55, 63, 69
Worcester
 Goods Engine shed 19

Yoker 23